BORDER TOWNS

C. S. GISCOMBE

BORDER TOWNS

DALKEY ARCHIVE PRESS

Library of Congress Cataloging-in-Publication Data

Names: Giscombe, C. S., 1950-
Title: Border towns / C. S. Giscombe.
Description: First edition. | Champaign : Dalkey Archive Press, 2016. |
    Contains essays, criticism, and other prose writings.
Identifiers: LCCN 2014029967 | ISBN 9781564789983 (softcover :
acid-free paper)
Classification: LCC PS3557.I78 A6 2016 | DDC 818/.54--dc23
LC record available at http://lccn.loc.gov/2014029967

Partially funded by a grant by the Illinois Arts Council, a state agency

www.dalkeyarchive.com
Victoria, TX / McLean, IL / Dublin

Dalkey Archive Press publications are, in part, made possible through
the support of the University of Houston-Victoria and its program in
creative writing, publishing, and translation.

Cover: Photo by Anita Noemi Garza

CONTENTS

Some of these pieces appeared previously in print—often in different form—in the following journals and collections: *A Poetics of Criticism* (edited by Kristin Prevallet, Pam Rehm, Juliana Spahr, and Mark Wallace), *American Book Review* (Charles B. Harris), *Angles of Ascent* (Charles Rowell), *Beauty is a Verb* (Jennifer Bartlett, Sheila Black, and Michael Northern), *Black Nature* (Camille Dungy), *Boog City* (Arielle Greenberg and David Kirschenbaum), *Brick* (Michael Ondaatje and Linda Spalding), *Chain* (Jena Osman and Juliana Spahr), *Cottonwood Review* (Paul Hotvedt), *Diverse Landscapes: Re-reading Place Across Cultures in Contemporary Canadian Writing* (Karin Beeler and Dee Horne), *The Encyclopedia Project* (Tisa Bryant), *Harriet Blog* (Mark Nowak), *O-blek* (Peter Gizzi and Connell McGrath), *PhillyTalks Series* (Louis Cabri), *Poets on Teaching* (Joshua Marie Wilkinson), *Race, Romanticism, and the Atlantic* (Paul Youngquist), *Telling It Slant: Avant-Garde Poetics of the 1990s* (Steven Marks and Mark Wallace), *Tripwire* (David Buuck), *Viz.* (Roxi Power Hamilton), *What I Say* (Aldon Lynn Nielsen and Lauri Ramey), *XCP: Cross-Cultural Poetics* (Mark Nowak).

Early support from the Fund for Poetry, the Illinois Arts Council, and the National Endowment for the Arts encouraged and permitted my work on this book, as did two Faculty Research Grants—ten years apart—from the Canadian Embassy to the United States. Later, the Gorsebrook Research Institute at Saint Mary's University provided me with office space and conversation during an important extended stay in Halifax. A Humanities Research Fellowship from the University of California, Berkeley, allowed me to complete work on *Border Towns*. I'm grateful.

A NOTE

In June 2011 Madeline Giscombe—with whom this book ends—and I arrived by train from Sofia in Istanbul and two days later crossed the Bosporus into Asia on one of the ferries.

The mistake or the short-sightedness is to perceive border towns as finite or one-to-one compositions, or as places where monoliths stretch and mingle; or stare at one another. A traveler crosses water, say, and then everything is different and yet the same. "One feels the purifying change," or "a weightless change," or threatening-if-abstract change, but a change that is in some sense familiar or expected and that "makes sense." Perhaps at best is *border town*—the term—the gesture toward something that's actually untenable or untenably awkward.

I would offer that border towns are places where the range *starts*, or, perhaps better, that border towns are the most obvious sites of the range; border towns are in fact unstable—they're full of too much information, they're bursting. Even a traveler senses this.

To live in a border town—or to have such a place as one's town of origin—is something else.

Buffalo, Kansas City, Detroit, New Orleans, Tijuana, the Miami International Airport, Plattsburgh, Cape Vincent, Cincinnati, Nuevo Laredo, Panama City, Indianapolis, Harper's Ferry, the inevitable McDonald's restaurant at the marge of town where interstate and local strip intersect (the McDonald's itself only "another city of arrival and departure"), arguably Dayton, certainly Chicago, East St. Louis, Sault Ste. Marie, etc.

And Ralph Ellison's Invisible Man, who understood his living not in "the jungle of Harlem . . . but in a border area" to be a joke on the power company.

Between town and jungle, then. Swaths of town, the neighborhood over the tracks, "[w]ay over on my far side of the river,"

Back-of-the-Yards, "the problem of the color line." It's no overstate-
ment to note that color does inform all the categories: the experience
of the border has its origins in and takes its shapes from color.

To live or to have begun in "a border area" is a fact of conscious-
ness; and/or it is a strategy of reading that one carries into other
situations. It overlaps. Race or ethnicity and even national identity
are fluid in the grand schemes; but locally, crossing between certain
locations is a complicated act (or set of complicated actions) and
your stated destination—whether you think it matters or not—will
mark you just like your point of origin does.

It often seems to me that one of the best uses to which prose
can be put is describing poetry. Even so, the boundary between
prose and poetry is like *anything* else—you step across, sneak over,
migrate, "jump for England," are remitted, are bound over, extra-
dited, you make do. You overlap and persist and admit to every-
thing—you deny nothing but accept all designations.

Gloria Anzaldúa wrote:

The sea cannot be fenced,
el mar does not stop at borders.

The border as a fixed place or as a number of fixed places is false. It
"surfaces" at unlikely situations; it surfaces unexpectedly, it locates
itself. It does not summon you.

Opacity also has its colors. But these prose pieces, composed in
the latter half of the 1990s and the first dozen years of the twen-
ty-first century (and arranged here in more or less chronological
order), were written to document things other than their own shapes,
to engage topics other than range, naming, opacity, contradiction,
or "the shape of reference itself." Instead I name nothing here and
refer, if haphazardly, to everything in an effort at exposition.

At the end of this book I take pains to recall Madeline Giscombe's
and my excursion into the market stalls of England in the spring of
1987. The idea for our 2011 trip had been to ride the rails to the

end of Europe, to the border city of Istanbul—the trip framed neither country nor lament; and I claim no genius for the picaresque. Instead, we sang—with some abandon—the obvious song on station platforms as we waited for trains.

Berkeley, September 2013

BORDER TOWNS

873 WORDS ON WHERE THINGS GO / STATEMENT FOR *O·BLEK*

Canada, I'd said at the end of my first book, *was further North than we'd imagined.*

And in the second, of the same place (of, specifically, the St. Lawrence): *the first edge / of the great covenant / with space // the* arrangement *// into here / & whatever lies beyond the gestures / in its direction.*

In the third: *I dreamed I saw us on the coast // wading in the Atlantic off Senegal, off Gambia, // the coast of beautiful Gabon or Cameroon, I couldn't tell, // but there were white people on the cliffs above us // the pale voices clearly phrased in the wind // at our backs as usual & waking I saw it had been the dunes on Lake Ontario I saw, // that we'd been at the end of Rte 414, at the end of upstate N.Y., // that it was Canada across the water, // more ambiguous than we'd thought for an archetype // all invisible etc. to be so big.*

The fourth book, the poetry-book-in-progress now, is *about* Canada.

The title of this document's "poetics for Gizzi & them"—had to save it as *something* on this drive and so without effort or particular thought went right into the voice of my childhood in among the first generation of people born in the North. And gestured as well at the correspondence from Peter Gizzi and Juliana Spahr, inviting me to the New Coast poetry festival at Buffalo. "Where you goin'?" "With Gizzi and them." (And have apologized to Ms. Spahr, for having turned her into the plural third person—Gizzi was the name I'd heard before and so it clicked.) For years I thought I myself had been born down in Birmingham, that "my mother bore me in the Southern wild" (to hell with the little English boy). But I was born in fact, as we'd all or mostly been, in Ohio, parents from Dixie. They were the last wave of the great migration: North. The archetype, perhaps *its* birth or, more correctly (since the archetype is *old*), its coincidence with my birth, my coming up.

No point though in trying to face it (the archetype, North) in language or any other way as some destiny (peculiar, racial, magical, some easy metaphor)—rather my interest is making use of knowledge about the geographical situation: where one is situated in relation to geographic entities (streets, rivers and bridges, embankments, sides of quite real tracks) and coming to terms with that: a poetic of situation(s), reference, notation, placement. In "The Changing Same," Baraka said something about "the slick city people we become after the exodus." The reference is to what happened "when the Negro left the land" (as Baldwin put it in *The Fire Next Time*). I'm wanting to use the represented edge(s) of the city as the other intelligence—beyond the native or alongside it—which is the one the poem lives in. Feeds on? Becomes?

I find myself these days at work on—in addition to poetry—a book of autobiographical travel essays which seemed to me at first to be at odds with poetry. But it's possible to see them, the essays, as description not *of* the poem but of where I was when I was making it: that the motion through landscape—the motion's terribly specific but unnamable in a clear-eyed prose breakdown—is, OK, "the poem" and that the essay is a simpleminded map (to paraphrase an M. Atwood narrator) to where a vision could be had, not necessarily to the vision itself.

Though vision itself is a synthesis, a mixed bag, a merger. John Morgan's "Libra" poem from *Intersections*: "'The cells try to come to terms with the site.'" (Quoting a radio broadcast.) But the first poem I saw anyone *make* was in sixth grade. Our teacher, an unconscionably racist lady of no discernible intellect, could never recollect the name of our classmate, Steveson Moore, and said one day out of that exasperation, "I always want to call you Sylvester"—to which Steveson Moore replied, in that first-generation-growing-up-in-the-North lilt, "I always want to call *you* Dick and Jane," thus marrying

with some precision the most ostentatiously banal named aspect of
all our lives in that school—our experience thus far in our progress
North—to that lady, the representative on earth of those who would
perpetrate such banality on us or any group of humans.

Didn't he synthesize? Revising her statement by repeating it
and taking the proper names of those two literary incorporeals and
making 'em into a title that was at once definitive and significantly
destructive (meaning explosive though the parameters of said explo-
sion were lost on her). My boy came to *terms* with the conditions; or
he brought terms to them. He made the conditions look, or *sound*,
like him, like all of us. Didn't he deftly transform that innocent little
effort to take his name?

My book-in-progress is about specifically black names—specifi-
cally this one, Giscombe or Giscome—up there in Canada.

The poem as geographic statement of situation. "The path traced
by a moving point." The poem faces North as it moves into and out
of situations, speaking to 'em in a language of site-specifics.

BORDER TOWNS, BORDER TALK

The likeliest path is one traced by the money, "a kind of poetry."

John Robert Giscome, born in Jamaica in the penultimate year of slavery there, goes the story, went to Panama as a young man to work on the railroad across the isthmus, which was the shortest—meaning here "most economical"—way for Americans to get from east-coast U.S. to west, which is where the gold was in those days. And back again. It was Colonel George Totten's railroad and the colonel built it along with his partner, Mr. John Trautwine, in the years of the California Rush. (They were followed many years later by Mr. George Washington Goethals and his canal, and the tracks are gone now, underwater.) Once there, John R. Giscome and all the other Jamaicans and Chinese men as well built the broad-gauge line on which Americans rode in bearable comfort back and forth between the oceans. But then, on he went to California himself, goes the story, to look for the gold himself: he found a fair amount of it not in California but in the Cassiar up in B.C. and he died rich in Victoria (where the *Colonist*, reporting on his death, described him as "the aged [small N] negro" but praised him as "a man worthy of honor and respect" and termed him "a pioneer") and, that way, out-lived his projected mortality as a railroad worker and outdistanced his own description as part of the collective "West Indian labour": he got all outside the lines that geography, race, and the languages of white people had made for him. He spoke lines not scripted for him and, that way, was not a "pioneer" or even a "creole"—he was neither of those words. He became, instead, a confusion in the talk of others, he became the presence of qualification and the demand for compound sentences of description, a symbol of that for which there is no symbol or image, "the figure of outward."

In television documentaries we have talking heads. Joseph Schott (identified by subtitle as author of *Rails Across Panama*) talking about the hellish burg that greeted the gentlemen who came to build the railroad: "Panama City was two centuries old and had 8,000 to 10,000 permanent inhabitants, 2,000 of whom could be classified as 'white' by adopting a very loose definition of the term." And Mr. Schott again, quoting an old French pamphlet that said of the Panama Railroad, "It is said that upon the railway of the Isthmus . . . there is buried a Chinaman under each crosstie," failing to understand the uses of metaphor, saying that this was "completely untrue" and calculating 140,000 crossties to which he triumphantly compares the sum total—1,000—of Chinese workers ever employed. Linda Eversole (formerly with the Heritage Conservation Branch) notes, though, that 2,000 Jamaicans were employed on the project by 1854. And a promo for a CBC double feature: *The Treasure of the Sierra Madre* followed by *Surfacing*. A cut from the first film: in the Dormitorio with its name, El Oso Negro, in fading paint on the wall behind them, Walter Huston, himself a prospector, telling Bogart that he, Huston, "never knew a prospector who died rich." The hotel's name, The Black Bear, is both that and a specific spot of untranslated language—*Negro*, with its long English E, *knee-grow*—on the backdrop but nothing as far as the movie goes except *part* of that backdrop, of no consequence to the movie's plot or even to the moment here reproduced between the partners that passed underneath it like it was a herald or something. (More on *Surfacing* later.)

The waves coming west and north next, after the gold rush, were, arguably, pioneers, a word that has, like "creole," multiple meanings, a different one for every obituary in every newspaper. But what is in some ways standard is the implicit investment "pioneer" has in people beyond or behind the pioneer himself—ancestors, descendants, dependents, representatives of the little tyrannies culture is—and as well an undercurrent of perceived, feared instability tarted up into

something respectable, at least in the mouths of describers blabbing
through their own uneasiness, young newspapermen losing their
youths to the creeping understanding of the uncertainty of anything,
facts or no facts: one comes around the long curve and comes up
on "nothing that is not there and the nothing that is." Pioneer's a
hedge against the uncertainty, against the wild cards in someone's
family, broadly defined here to mean the spate of transcendent yet
personal identities we like to see marching alongside us through life,
the "familiar"—"traditional family values," touted the Republicans
on TV. Anyway, *Land, a Living and Wealth: The Story of Farming
and Social Conditions in Western Canada* was an attractive, up-to-
the-minute pamphlet (in Arts & Crafts Movement design) put
out by the Grand Trunk Pacific in 1913. Ernest Camcroft's article
therein said: "The G.T.P. is the latest racial trek. The engineers of
the National Transcontinental are racing Goethals of the Culebra
Cut to the Pacific." The noun's from Afrikaans, a real Boer word,
trek, rendering the adjective—*racial*—redundant, an example of
overemphasis rendered, I reckon, in the service of the message going
un-missed under any circumstance of reading. The whiteness of the
white man on the move is most white. It's OK, bring your families,
come, we're all going.

Another estimation, from the redoubtable Bruce Ramsey, from
that man's book, *Ghost Towns of B.C.*: Tête Jaune Cache was "British
Columbia's Sodom and Gomorrah during the construction of the
Grand Trunk Pacific Railway," he says and then goes on and quotes
someone named J. A. Lower in an old *B.C. Historical Quarterly*: "A
special selection of shacks grew up at the western end of the pass
on the site of the Tête Jaune Cache Indian village. An old Negress
ran the town . . . an 'end of steel' village is a disgrace but Tête Jaune
was indescribable."

The end of steel is the place where the tracks stop, if tempo-
rarily; the villages, according to Lower, are three miles past that
point, along the line down which the tracks will extend. End of
steel as *phrase* has all the obvious metaphoric values, but I'm drawn

to the example of disgrace: that "an old Negress ran the town." Where was she from? The dug is withered from the chest. Or perhaps not. Comes the matter of what breast suckled Sir James Douglas, first governor of the province. W. Kaye Lamb—also in the *Quarterly*—says: "It has been stated that [James Douglas's mother] was a mulatto, largely on the authority of Letitia Hargrave, who referred to James Douglas himself as a mulatto in a letter written in 1842. But Mrs. Hargrave scarcely knew Douglas himself. John Tod, a much better witness, since he knew Douglas well over a long term of years, stated that James Douglas's mother was a [capital c] Creole. This is a very different term, and does not necessarily carry any implication of mixed blood. It simply means that she was born in the West Indies, or in some other similar tropical region." The governor was born in Guyana, up on the shoulder of South America that hunches along the Caribbean. The *OED*'s largely supporting of Mr. Lamb, so much so that I figure he consulted it: the authors are quite specific—"the name having no connotation of colour"—as though in anticipation of that question or perhaps in response to a common misperception. The definition notes parenthetically that some eighteenth-century writers attribute the first instances of the word's use to "South American negroes [who applied it] to their own children born in America." Among white people the term Creole seems to be, according to the dictionary, most often applied to those families that are in some sense or tradition Spanish.

Twenty years later Robin Winks said: "His knowledge that his mother was either a West Indian mulatto or a Creole obviously increased his concern." This an estimation of the governor's welcoming of the California black immigrants in '59. At that long moment annexation by the U.S. was a credible threat, as they say, and Douglas had wanted the province to look big and full of people with no particular allegiance to the U.S. The black exodus to Victoria was a middle-class move—the people who came were in business or owned property and who figured they deserved, because of that, better than what they were getting. And there was Douglas out at the end of a dock, said someone in a poem, "welcoming, Creole, pragmatic."

Now Governor Douglas is the first photo in Garbette A. M. Garraway's pamphlet, *Accomplishments and Contributions: A Handbook on Blacks in British Columbia*. He's tall and uncomfortable looking, muttonchopped and light skinned in the rather formal portrait. On the page he is what Lowell said of Colonel Shaw's statue on Boston Commons: "he seems to wince at pleasure / and suffocate for privacy." Impossible to know quite what he looked like in the flesh. The caption calls him "a West Indian of racially mixed parentage" but in the text she calls his mother "'Creole.'" She places the C-word in quotes, which act I translate as a broad wink on her part, a nod to an understanding of its ambiguity. But even "ambiguity" is a euphemism. Her associations make me think Ms. Garraway's black, and I think she's self-aware and she means, I think, that Creole is a polite way of saying "mixed," which itself translates rather easily into "black."

On A&E last year, 1994, the segment of *The Real West* on Canada. I was in a motel room in Indianapolis, Indiana stretched out on the bed with the god-box in my hand and suddenly there were people from B.C. talking about places I'd been. Apparently some of the controversy about Governor Douglas's blood is over. Kenny Rogers, the narrator, intoned that the governor had created in B.C. "a new society, one he would ever hold himself above." In explanation of this on came Minister of Small Business, Tourism and Culture Bill Barlee's head to think aloud: "I think it went back to his childhood. He *was* half black, I think he felt that; his wife was half Indian, I think he felt that as well. So to make up for that he was a royal personage in B.C." I was in Indianapolis interviewing for a job I didn't want at the poor-relation urban campus of Indiana University. But I'd been interested in the city because of its big black population, including a real middle class: it's a *first* city, meaning here it's a viable destination for people coming up north over the Mason-Dixon Line and that makes it a border town, a place of influx and mystery, an ambiguous town, one that has *so many* halves that nothing ever has to be made up for, or even could be.

I grew up in a place like that, in a city in southern Ohio. As children we taunted, "Your mama's so black that when she go to night school they mark her absent"; or "Your mama's lips so big she use Chapstick in a spray bottle." But Langston Hughes said that when white people say Does your color rub off? the best reply is, "Ask your mama." Much of *Menace II Society* pivots on the early "innocent" speech by an immigrant grocer about the protagonist's mother and how he pities her for having a son such as the protagonist, an act for which the protagonist shoots the grocer dead and this murder sets the plot in progress. But it's not the insult to the protagonist himself that gets things going: it's that the grocer "talked about my mama." It's a very funny moment in the movie—if we can define "funny" as a recognition that the audience must have and which the character on the screen is ignorant of as he or she high-steps blithely into harm's way. It's profoundly high comedy, even if it's a bit heavy. Stories often are. Stories come down alongside "history," which Henry Kissinger calls "the memory of States." Stories exist in the other service, as "blows against the empire." In the *tradition* there's this story about President Harding: a white man had married the president's aunt and had gone happily about his domestic business. But then one day one of his neighbors, also white, taunted him in such a way that inspired him to thwack the fellow on the head with a piece of iron, which led to his demise—that man had ridiculed him for having married a "nigger"; he went to trial for it, the defense claiming justifiable homicide, so grievous was the slander, but it didn't work because the jury found that "the Hardings were always so called." The blue-eyed man in the dock went to jail. White people don't know this story or the other ones about Warren Harding's "mixed blood" and his sister, the well-known colored policewoman in Washington, D.C.[1]

---

1 J. A. Rogers includes a section on Harding in the second volume of *Sex and Race*; much of his material comes, apparently, from William Estabrook Chancellor's pamphlet, *Warren Gamaliel Harding, President of the United States*, published in Dayton in 1922. The

"A woman's a two-face," goes the old song. Your mama wears two faces, one black, one white. They blur and become a single face, a black one. Thylias Moss, revising Robert Frost's "Stopping by Woods . . ." and making her own poem out of it, talking about the promise a black girl makes to her face: "that it not be mistaken as shadow."

But Tête Jaune himself! After whom the disgraceful,

---

pamphlet—available online in 2015—purports to prove that some of Harding's ancestors were black; the evidence comes from interviews with older white Ohioans, people in some sense "native" to Marion, Morrow, and Crawford Counties. Early in the pamphlet Chancellor writes,

> We agree that they have the right to ask to be considered white because racially they are mostly white; but we deny that they have the right to assert the lie that they have always been considered and have always considered themselves white. We assert that the rest of us have the right to ask whether they have had the rearing of white men and women. We assert the right of American neighbors of these Hardings to pass upon their qualifications social and moral and intellectual to be treated as all-white persons are. Pure white is not colored and is the opposite of negro. It is something that cannot be claimed without being questioned.

Of Harding's grandmother, Chancellor wrote, "She was so dark that she frightened white children of her neighbors."

In 2015 the *New York Times*, citing the results of DNA testing on a number of Harding descendants, came up with a more or less definitive response. "The tests found 'no detectable genetic signatures of sub-Saharan African heritage in any of the three cousins,' said Julie Granka, a population geneticist at AncestryDNA." AncestryDNA is "a service" of the popular Ancestry.com website.

But earlier, in 2008, in the months leading up to Barack Obama's first election, the *Times* had published a less "definitive" article on the Chancellor book—and the rumors of Harding's ancestry—by Beverly Gage. She wrote, "To anyone who tracks it down today, Chancellor's book comes across as a laughable partisan screed, an amalgam of bizarre racial theories, outlandish stereotypes and cheap political insults. But it also contains a remarkable trove of social knowledge—the kind of community gossip and oral tradition that rarely appears in official records but often provides clues to richer truths."

James Wright's "Two Poems About President Harding" (1963) concludes thus:

America goes on, goes on
Laughing, and Harding was a fool.
Even his big pretentious stone
Lays him bare to ridicule.
I know it. But don't look at me.
By God, I didn't start this mess.
Whatever moon and rain may be,
The hearts of men are merciless.

African-mothered village, after whom the Yellowhead Highway looping up past the turnoff to Giscome, B.C. The bright yellow signs pace the road out to the Alberta line, the gesture back east. "Tête Jaune was indescribable," says Lower meaning the village. Father Morice, always teacherly, says: "A yellow-haired trapper (*tête jaune* being the French for yellow head) was responsible for its name, as that Indian, who was an Iroquois, used to cache or put up in a temporary store or shelter the furs he had procured in those mountain fastnesses. The scenery in that pass is 'grand and striking beyond description . . .'" The priest disappears into the thurible swing of his quotation marks (into the language of Milton and Cheadle's expedition) to get beyond the description of Pierre Bostonais, the person the Akriggs identify as having been called Tête Jaune. We depart from the colors his body was into the *indescribable* once again and find refuge in language that tells us that language can't do it, can't match, can't dance, can't scale, etc. It is, like the flesh, weak, but weak in different ways: perhaps its weakness cannot match that of the flesh. Take me to the place—a song might go, rising—the place along the highway, through the indescribable pass named after the miscegenation and *not* to the miscegenation itself. It's to that very describable pass that we don't go.

So what's the origin of Pierre Bostonais's yellow head? Is he the product of a kidnap story, a captivity tale in which the maiden's dragged unwillingly out into the nightscape by savages, perhaps as a child, and made to live under *conditions* until she accepts them and takes, finally, willingly, a savage for a "husband"? Or is he the child of a plantation novel in which the father was a white man—as the family name, Bostonais, might suggest—who found his own women too frail for his appetites and so crossed the color line or a color line, shucking off civilization as he shucked off his clothes to do the nasty with a sultry dark-skinned babe. Was little Pierre a recrimination as was the function of that "strange blue-eyed Negro" in one of Carson McCullers's gothic morality tales? All such stories exist as specters and offer threat and menace (and something else unnamable in a family newspaper or pamphlet) to our pioneers.

By 1913 the end of steel had reached Giscome Station and John R. Giscome had been dead for six years.

In 1863 he and his partner, the Bahamian Henry McDame, were showed, by Indians, a way over the Continental Divide between the Fraser River and Summit Lake, northeast of Fort George. A newspaper account—from the 15 December issue of the *Colonist*—survives: they were on their big year-long prospecting trip into the Peace River Country from Quesnel and, about forty miles northeast of the place where the Salmon, which was running high that year, comes into the Fraser, "they made a portage of about 9 miles to a lake, leaving the canoes behind." At that lake—now Summit Lake—they picked up another canoe and ascended the Crooked River, getting eventually to McLeod's Lake. They visited the H.B. Company Fort there, "where a salute of about 20 shots was fired, with firearms, in honor of the arrival of that party through that route which had never been traversed by any others than Indians." The paper couldn't really have used the more economical and common phrase, "never been traversed by white men," which I'm sure most readers imagined anyway when they got to that line "never been traversed *by any others than Indians*": it's a quite reasonable choice of words, really, and would have been even if Giscome and McDame *had* been white. But knowing our lads were African puts a spin onto the thing—it *foregrounds* their position, makes it both less and more than a blurry near-occasion at the margin of the picture, something other than the familiar white men / Injuns racial dichotomy. McDame and Giscome had actually originally left Quesnel in November of 1862, but they got caught by the ice on the Fraser and had to winter in Fort George, setting out for real in April of '63 and making it over the Rocky Mountain Portage in July—there, in the country over there, some days, the partners "would see as many as a dozen bears on the banks of the river."

So John Robert Giscome returned to Victoria near Christmas, bringing samples of volcanic rock from the place at the confluence

of the Red Deer and Smoky Rivers and profound news of "good dig-
gings found." The article appeared under the headline "Interesting
from the Rocky Mountains." Linda Eversole says she thinks John R.
Giscome wrote it himself but it does appear as an as-told-to tale—all
about "our informant"—there on the front page. The rest is history,
meaning indisputable amounts of money were spent—the Giscome
Portage begins appearing on maps in 1871, the year the citizens
of Quesnel petitioned the government for $10,000 to construct a
"waggon road" across it so that they could proceed more efficiently
toward the Omineca, where yet another gold rush was starting up:
it was a way in and it was a way over the hump as well—it went over
the Divide, it crossed between the Arctic Watershed and the Pacific
Watershed. Water was at either end, a geophysical idea of water as
furthest arm or grasp of particular ocean. The Giscome Portage was
another way between the oceans; it's on most of the maps for those
fifty years when things moved by water, before the Hart Highway,
before the Pacific Great Eastern Railway; and when the Grand Trunk
Pacific line came through from the east they named Giscome Station
for it because it was close to the famous portage. The town's situated
at the western end of Eaglet Lake and it prospered for a long time
because of the big sawmill there—a weekly newspaper, dances, a
movie theater, competing stores, a famous nightspot which perched
way above town. The mill closed in 1975 and most of the town
disappeared and the houses were bulldozed by the company. But
people still live there.

* * *

In 1964 Bruce Ramsey wrote a piece called "John Giscome's
Country," apparently as a special supplement for the *Giscome News*.
The first three paragraphs are worth quoting in their entire length:

> In the passing parade of B.C.'s exciting history, there march
> before our eyes many men and women whose names for a brief

moment are indelibly stamped in the record and then, just as quickly as they appeared, they pass from our ken.

Such a man was John Giscome (sometimes spelled Giscombe) after whom the townsite and post office serving the Eagle Lake Sawmills was named. We see him in the midst of one of the greatest gold stampedes the world has ever known; we see him engaged in back-breaking toil, sometimes in vain, and at times riding the crest of success. We see him for fleeting moments in the Cariboo, in the Rocky Mountain Trench, in the Peace River country, and beyond to the spreading prairies. And then we lose sight of him forever.

We know nothing of his activities until 1862 when he headed out of the infant Quesnellemouth, now Quesnel. Some writers in the post-Giscome era have described him as being a Negro but there is no concrete evidence on which to hand this decision. His partner was Henry McDame, a Negro from the Bahamas and, at one time, Giscome Portage was known as "Nigger Portage," but whether this was because of Giscome or McDame is not recorded. The claim he worked on McDame Creek, with Henry, was sometimes called the "Negro Claim." And, so, it is all circumstantial evidence as to his racial background.

Mr. Ramsey's qualification in these paragraphs is matched by his equivocation, leading the reader to think that there may be something big at stake here. He's got a long list of books on historical topics and I'd imagine that he understands his profession to be historian, and I imagine further that he understands his role as that is to tell the rest of us how to feel about the stuff we've already heard about. I imagine he thinks about his *responsibility*. It's a professional job he does for the duration of the piece: in the following paragraphs not reproduced here he takes the narrative back to past perfect, back to the past before the past, back to Mackenzie and Simon Fraser, quoting from the journals of those gentlemen; he then returns to the more recent past, revisiting Giscome and

McDame on whom he spends a page and a half excerpting from the account in the *Colonist* that I've excerpted up above, the one Linda Eversole maintains that John R. Giscome wrote. And because of that, Giscome and McDame's trip looks like, in form (in *status*), something similar to the travels of Mackenzie and Fraser. And it's called "John Giscome's Country." It's too late now not to think of men going out to seed the land as they claim it by penetrating it: it's a dangerous responsibility to identify the patron, the *patroon*, the father of this-and-that in whatever metaphors, the paternal figure on a horse—his benevolence, pioneering spirit, and sexuality inspiring endless admiration. It's a dangerous responsibility and the evidence for John Robert Giscome's blackness is suggested and weighed and it's McDame who gets identified in the lineup. McDame gets offered as the sacrificial woolly-head, the true undoubted blood, the one on whom the blackness of all the descriptions can definitely be blamed, and Giscome gets off; he *walks*—as they say in the cop shows on TV—because the "evidence," Bruce Ramsey says, is "circumstantial" and because the perpetrator or at least a perpetrator has been identified. Bruce Ramsey helps us presume the man's innocence, presume that he wasn't black until it's proven otherwise. His not being *necessarily* black means all the things named for him in the Cariboo are not necessarily black either—what fathers do is put their names on things and people, put their blood into people. People spend money to search out their fathers, for down through the father come goods and rank and privilege. Words like heritage and birthright pop up. This is the heritage, O my brothers and cousins in Canada: this is what's hidden in the blood.

In Linda Eversole's research about John R. Giscome she found herself in touch by mail with an apparently white woman from Winnipeg who was descended from people who lived in Jamaica in the nineteenth century, including some Giscomes. I've always suspected that there were some upset white people in the '70s, casualties of the genealogical craze that followed everybody watching *Roots* on TV. My guess is that some of those people trooping into county courthouses with their grandmother's Bible had to discover

that they were descended from African-Americans, had to find out
that they were descended from their own slaves. It's the great unsaid
thing (the discovery of an unexpected and unwanted forbear), an
experience that's rarely talked about, and I'd think it would be like,
for some people, having a child with a birth defect: I produced
that? *That* produced me? But Linda Eversole's informant was cool
about it: some time ago she'd found a pivotal ancestor in the welter
of couplings and begettings that was the planter class back then in
that place, a woman named Anne, and in 1991 she calmly received
the news of Anne's antecedents: "We have had no oral tradition of
Anne's being of black descent," she says in a letter, "however we do
have a tradition that there was Spanish in the family and this was
often used as a euphemism. I have always felt that one should be
aware that this possibility exists if one has island ancestry, and if you
don't want to know, don't investigate." Spanish? The Giscomes and
Giscombes were apparently always black—all of us I've ever met
or heard about or seen referred to have been people like me: black
people who have Jamaica in common with one another. When I
read from my poetry book *Giscome Road* people come up and ask
afterwards if I'm related to him. Possibly, but it's the pastiche I'm
wanting, the mingled commonality, the self existing alongside other
selves that are similar. But even then ethnicity and relation are acts
of will and not birthrights. And they're acts of generosity, acts of
inclusion. African-Americans, who have had no birthright for the
generations here in Babylon, have understood this for a while now.
The culture has demanded transformative powers of us; we suffer
no illusions about the purity of our forebears or their centrality or
about the centrality and purity of anybody else's ancestry either.[2]

---

2 Ancestral purity, or the lack thereof, has been a site in the U.S. for both discussions
of racism and shorings-up of it as an institution. Some of both kinds of discourse can
be found in popular or semi-popular films of the last several years. The actor Charlton
Heston has often been cast in films with complicated racial "messages" or motifs, includ-
ing miscegenation. It's possible and tempting, for example, to read his discovery of "his
destiny" at the end of *Planet of the Apes* as a racist re-evocation of America (as opposed to,
or along with, Africa) being a version of "the white man's grave." But another cinematic

We're always a town at the margin, a town at the edge of town where the exchanges take place. There's nothing at the center—the heart's empty, it's the nothing. We improvise, we invent.

Likewise does the speaker in *Surfacing*—marginal, disinvolved, *valued*—attempt to invent an identity or synthesize one out of elements in her past. I've argued before for the book's being a quest for a specifically non-white Canadian identity but this year I'm reading it as a problematization of the ideas clustered around paternity. The readings aren't really opposed—both have to do with disappearing into the nothingness of the past. The speaker's missing father notes, early into things, that "[there's] nothing in the north but the past and not very much of that either." The movie version they showed on CBC is insistently about nothing but its own shrillness, a disappointment after *Treasure of Sierra Madre*.

(I was living in Vancouver in an "illegal suite" with cable TV, 1991. I was writing a poetry book called *Giscome Road*, about northern places, and I decided to bicycle, as an act of physical homage, the five hundred miles from Vancouver to Giscome, B.C. I took my American edition of *Surfacing* with me, having begun rereading it after having seen the awful movie version. I read it in my tent at night, by flashlight.)

---

event, *The Omega Man* (based loosely on Richard Matheson's undervalued 1950s novel *I Am Legend*), found Heston romantically involved with a canny black woman who gave in to the pressure from the hordes in the streets and "reverted" to vampirism—reversion, the avatar rising in the tainted blood, is a common motif in the horror film genre and reflects, to my reading, an unstated preoccupation on the part of filmmakers and public with miscegenation and its "effects." Border towns are also, because of their geographical situation, a site for miscegenation as metaphor. The town sprawling over the U.S.-Mexican line in *Touch of Evil* is a case in point—it's constructed largely of sexual threat; the filmmakers in this case, however, seem quite aware of what they're up to. The film is also *about* the film noir genre and achieves a postmodern quality with its running gags, the bizarre presences of Marlene Dietrich and Dennis Weaver, and its celebration of Janet Leigh's very white breasts in gigantic white brassieres in conjunction with gangs of leering dark-skinned boys. Charlton Heston himself, his skin darkened for his role as—in the words of costar Orson Welles—"some kinda Mexican," is the *familiar* threat: the scene cut from the original film involves Leigh's attempted seduction of him, a scene with strong sexual content and one in which the camera highlights, in conjunction with that, the differences in the colors of the two stars' skins.

In the novel, the woman's father had marked a map with Xs, which she took to be the locations of pictographs. Following the map she located one site, finding the described flat rock, the cliff's blank face, and figured the thing should be painted there, faded. She'd imagined it would be "a word and not its meaning." But there was nothing there.

She said later, "Why talk when you *are* a word?" and declared herself a "place." But she was nowhere.

A totem elects itself here, for here: she gardens and watches for her father to improbably appear or reappear, unrecognizable. At the bottom of the page what comes is a bear: "It materialized on the path, snuffling along bulky and flat-footed, an enormous fanged rug."

When John R. Giscome died he left his money to his landlady Ella Cooness, who took it to Saltspring Island—offshore, unhidden—on which black people had unmysteriously appeared in 1857. She left it to the hospital there, at Ganges.

When I got to Giscome for the first time ever, on my English bicycle, I had no paper with me except for the blank pages at the end of *Surfacing*. On the "Writing the North" panel at UNBC, I held up my blue American edition open to those pages, saying, "See, an actual northern text!"

"A bright day, full of diffuse, centerless light," I'd written there, at Giscome, which was itself no destiny, no mother lode. And, further, "This *is* a place, we decided last night, but there's nothing here. Wch was right & wrong: what's here is the intersection of the railroad, the one the road makes, and whatever business CN has here—the 4 gondolas on a siding down there; the school &, most important, the view *out* from here.

"This feels to me like the empty center of the continent today."

FUGITIVE

Suppose a woman or a man was in "some sort of trouble."

Suppose that woman (or the man) was white and well connected, professional, which would put her (or him) at odds with being in trouble, speaking in terms of the narrative of tradition.

(All traditions are sexist. Rather many are racist. What about narrative?)

Suppose it was a man then, still white, still professional, how would you feel? Suppose he was just a white actor, playing us (though not playing *one* of us), suppose that.

"If a man was in some sort of trouble" and still "would be willing to come forward" now and again even if he'd had to "change his identity" and "toil"; or if he knew someone who was "relentless" and yet others who "were willing to help him, even lie for him"—then *what*? *What* then? Compared to *what*?

* * *

There was promise and, later on, an almost natural letdown around a TV show, an old series from the early '60s called *The Fugitive*: the promise—what *seemed* to be happening and so, for a long period, was happening—was endless expansion and accumulation with no particular regard to narrative structure (only the briefest and most token attention was paid to this by the show's producers): what we saw instead of such a structure was the suggestion of an infinite articulation—not "utterance or enunciation" but something like the way those long steam locomotives were jointed to take curves. Nor is this about wistful agrarianism, *that* fugitive, though Kimble, the title character, often took farmworker jobs. This is more about, say, Tracy Chapman singing the chorus to "Fast Car." Ms. Chapman's whole song's about being in trouble and being there is appropriate

or at least discernible (which is likely the reason that "Fast Car"
was popular). Where else *is* there to be, especially if you're honest?
What else is there to do but run? On the other hand there's the old
song "Nowhere to Run": the lyrics, "Nowhere to run to, baby /
Nowhere to hide," are patently untrue, a *lie*, title and chorus too—
there's *always* somewhere to run and somewhere to hide though
those places must be, often, invented. Yet the *song*'s not dishonest:
because of the sheer—meaning precipitous—strength and sound
of Martha Reeves's voice the song achieves a virtual truth, one that
surpasses the arguable lie of the lyrics. Willful performance'll *do* that
to absolute value. It's Martha Reeves's voice that makes everything
true, everything she ever *said* is the truth. Tracy Chapman sounds,
unfortunately, sweet, like Joni Mitchell at mid-career. Who do you
believe? Who *looks like* they're telling the thing beyond the story,
telling it the way it is, which hasn't got a thing to do with some
story and its closure? Who's willing? Who's willing to get further
on and deeper in trouble? Words and music, that music and those
words. Even old deep-image James Wright, who was often in trou-
ble himself, knew enough to step outside of himself and quote Judy
Holliday saying, "Well, look, honey, where I come from, when a girl
says she's in trouble, she's in trouble." The epigraph for his poem
"Trouble."

* * *

Some day in May 1991, nine o'clock in the morning and I was
sitting on the front porch with my shirt off reading an article by
Henry Giroux about indeterminacy, other-ness vs. the assertion of
the marginalized subject, black feminist models, etc. I'd started the
article at seven thirty or so and by nine I was nearly done with it
and sick of it too. It was full of typographical mistakes and written
in some man's voice, one of those that privileges difficulty, right? In
spite of that Giroux was proving to me he was smart, but he sure
does privilege contortion too without the authority of the dance,
without the dance giving his thing *any* authority.

I was in a seminar that my employer, Illinois State University, was paying for, about ways to incorporate multicultural perspectives into the classroom. The seminar leader was a white antiracist from the Ozarks, a local player in the new critical theory which certainly looks—if you read it carefully enough to pick out the paradigms— liberationist but which also looks (if you read it carefully enough to pick out the paradigms) careerist and power hungry and a way for young humanities academics to talk only to one another, stylish in their clothes and their serious faces in airports on their way to the MLA. The hegemony of all that. Fuck 'em if they can't take a joke. The packet our leader prepared for us was readings out of that tradition, that talk about authority and otherness and subject and object and discourse. Which *are* useful words, but then most words are useful, aren't they?

So every afternoon that hot week, including Memorial Day itself, we sat upstairs at the Multicultural Center and we beat that boy. (Which is what Ellison said, how Ellison talked about such talk and Ellison knew how to be useful and also how to dance. I'd taught *Invisible Man* that semester that had just ended, though I've never taught it well, and that novel was in my head then, as a series of overlays, as a series of lenses, as a series of illuminations.)

Nine o'clock every morning *The Fugitive* comes on A&E.

It was a show I'd watched as a child growing up in Dayton, Ohio, where Ralph Ellison had lived for a while. The earliest episodes are from 1963, presumably the season that began in September, like school did. I was in seventh grade that year, which was the year they shot the president. My grandmother had been in a supermarket when it was announced and she said that some of the white men who'd been working there began laughing and joking about it. I think she was the one from whom I first heard "they" used to describe who did it, even though it was widely assumed and believed back then that it had been old Lee Harvey Oswald acting, as the phrase goes, alone. They's singular, *e pluribus unum*, baby, ain't that what it means on the dime, the quarter, and the penny?

All the earliest episodes of *The Fugitive* start the same way, with a recap of the plot, of what's at stake here. Richard Kimble, a doctor (played by David Janssen), is on his way by train to Death Row. He's handcuffed to a police detective named Gerard (played by Barry Morse) and is awkwardly, because of the cuffs, smoking a cigarette. Dr. Kimble was convicted of killing his wife but of course he didn't really do it: the voice-over goes, "The irony? Richard Kimble is innocent," and goes on to say that just before our man found the murdered wife he saw a one-armed man—more on this later—"running from the scene." But then there's a train wreck—"Fate," goes the voice, "moves its huge hand"—and in the violence of that Kimble's handcuff is severed and he's off and running. Running from Gerard, searching after the one-armed man. (A light, superimposed from somewhere, makes a nova-like reflection on the metal of the broken handcuff as he runs, initially, from the wrecked train. Later episodes begin with a series of blurred freeze-frames of the train wreck and the voice-over intones "Reprieved by fate . . ." I guess someone thought that was better.)

Now as a child I'd watched it with great interest. For one thing, the tension was sustained from one episode to the next, and it was the same tension: I mean it always ended inconclusively, with a gesture out toward the highway, the forgivable cliché down which Kimble had to travel. Sometimes Gerard would appear, having had a tip that Kimble—traveling under one of his many Anglo-Saxon aliases—was in a certain place: there'd be a confrontation or almost-confrontation and Kimble would escape. Often the doctor was faced with dilemmas. Often the shows were sexy—in early episodes "loose," if confused and tragic, women would try without success to seduce Kimble and, now and again, in later episodes the producers would allow him to fuck and be fucked by a good, if tragic and confused, woman who wasn't exactly a "slut," this as the decade became The Sixties. And every once in a great while the one-armed man—played by Bill Raisch—would appear.

One could speak of fetishes, of Raisch's missing limb as one of these: that his arm ended incompletely (and that he rarely appears in the episodes) suggests various things, many of which are sexual, but then also there's the void that Kimble's always running into, a dangerous and continually retreating horizon, a place that doesn't really exist. Nowhere to run, nowhere to hide? This is some sort of trouble for sure, this is high trouble. (Raisch never wore a prosthesis on the show though he did "in real life," I read in an article in *TV Guide*. Something missing's more tantalizing, or so we could say.) In a Kirk Douglas vehicle, also from the '60s, the film *Lonely Are the Brave*, Bill Raisch played "that one-armed johnny" who gives Kirk Douglas a sound ass-kicking in a bar, early in the film, a pivotal scene because of the consequences.

(My father is a doctor and, back then, I was still entertaining notions of going into that field. I lost my own arm, the left one, as a result of an accident early in my childhood. I'm African-American, a phrase I like because the last two syllables of each word are the same and in that I see two near-identical dark faces; my mother said to write "American Negro" on a form for school, lecturing us that day in 1962 or 1963 on what that phrase implied. My friend Lamar Herrin was in *Lonely Are the Brave*; he had a bit part as a helicopter pilot and has stories about Kirk Douglas but none about Bill Raisch. These are facts to be brought up and gotten, as they say, past: they look like they're an offering but they're not. Nor do they explain much; they explain, in fact, rather little even though they hold *places* as places are held in a long line for, say, tickets. One becomes chummy with one's fellow line standers, this consequence of an accidental meeting.)

Kimble was a vector, a random set of directions, a loose anagram of trouble, kindle, tremble (David Janssen's weak chin), and kinship. Brother man, Kimble. He was upper class, white, professional, male.

Appearing with him now and again were a very young Greg Morris, Ivan Dixon, Ruby Dee once (as an African). Race was never mentioned and, truly, much was unsaid in these meetings, even in the music, which was the same insipidly elegiac horns and foreboding piano. In the lack of comment, though, the show turned: for young black viewers recognized those actors as the foils they were, but for Kimble's *blackness* (as opposed to his innocence or his upper-class origins which were themselves metaphors for his *whiteness*). And Kimble's blackness was a foil for the audience's own. These were the days before Bill Cosby and Robert Culp broke the color bar on TV and so such appearances were obviously important and anomalous at once. Kimble's blackness then was an act of discernment, an act of supreme metaphor, one that could be chanted endlessly and upon whose back one could ride on into the void with intent. Greg Morris and Ruby Dee were backup singers, exactly, to Kimble's HNIC, the Vandellas to his Martha Reeves. He'd *lost* his whiteness and for awhile it looked like he was never gonna get it back, like it was gone. He'd sing "Nowhere to Run, Nowhere to Hide," as he'd run and then as he'd hide. Kimble was the most important black presence then on episodic TV even though both he and David Janssen were white.

Kimble was Bigger Thomas; being a white man didn't stop him from being accused of and convicted of (which was so unlikely it had to be announced *each* week in the standard intro about irony and Fate) a black man's crime against, yes, property: "My wife," said Kimble over and over. E.g., (breathlessly) "They say I killed my wife and I couldn't prove my innocence." "Killed his wife?" said someone, interested, that music rising like eyebrows. Killed all y'all's wife. His crime was not his though the nightmare of the crime was everybody's: to stand like a black man in the dock and be sent away—up the river, or to Statesville, to Joliet, wherever they keep Ol' Sparky these days—because you sure as hell do *look* like you killed that lady, "their symbol of beauty," you look like that's your use, my brother, to stand there like that *to* get sent away forever. Some people never get to wake up from out of their nightmares.

So Kimble, a doctor, had "to toil at many jobs," as the intro says (which is the polite way of saying "work like a nigger," a phrase everyone's heard but which only some of the poorest white people, those who know most about working, would actually say) but then he got to wake up, regain his status, wake up, confront his one-armed nemesis. He and relentless, humorless Gerard closed in on and killed incomplete old Bill Raisch in the final episode. They closed up that void and later on in that same hour he got to, implicitly, fuck the very white, very squeaky clean "girl" from his home town, Stafford, Indiana (nicely, offscreen, presumably during the credits), this as an apparent reward for his sojourn in the netherworld of dark looks. Narrative kicks back in at the close. He got to complete things that way. He got to come in from out of the cold, from out of the make-it-up-as-you-go-along, from off his own vector. He got to stop being "in some sort of trouble" and become white himself, become white itself.

"Papa writes to Johnny"—goes the song from the '50s —"Johnny can't come home / Johnny can't come home / No Johnny can't come, / Papa writes to Johnny / Johnny can't come home / 'cause he's been on that chain gang too long." A man in some sorta trouble, he gotta keep *on*, but Kimble, he achieved closure, the aching disappointment of that, the betrayal. Even if it is natural, meaning *in the nature of*—it was, after all, TV.

* * *

The readings in our packet that summer were chosen to illuminate some theoretical bases for multiculturalism. Giroux, Spivak, Michael Awkward, Radhakrishnan, some others. Smart boys and girls but stiff, stiff, stiff. Is there a difference between stiffness and contortion? There's no rueful beauty in either one; no false step, no throwaway lines or jokes, fumbles and bungles. Nowhere to run, nowhere to hide? Nobody I read much wanted to run down to the rocks to hide his or her face. Without that desire—the intimation of being in trouble—there's no way the rocks can rejoin, *No hiding place*. I suggested near the end of the week that many of these theoretical multicultural bases had been covered rather well forty years ago by *Invisible Man*—the brilliant talk about history, e.g., that

follows Tod's death—and that made one of my fellows try to get
all hegemonic and say that that, as a novel, was not our discourse
as university professors. Which caused the other black member of
the seminar and me to jump up and, gesturing toward the packet,
declare more or less in unison, "This ain't my discourse," threatening
to *be* trouble and come forward *that* way. (We have some temper-
amental things in common, she and I, things beyond the obvious
blackness—maybe an unwillingness to be relentless, to close in.)

I don't mean to be confessional here but do you love me? Now?
That I can dance?

The Fugitive looks like other things but is not them.

(There's a movie version that'll be out soon, coming-this-sum-
mer, with strong-featured Indiana Jones as Dr. Kimble. I read about
it in *Trains* magazine. The credible threat of endless episodes being
shrunk down to two hours, made into a parenthesis for a rainy
summer afternoon. Will it articulate trouble, contradict itself and
understand and misunderstand invisibility, be excessive and in that
way lead to the palace of wisdom? Bargain matinees before six p.m.)

The Fugitive resembles *Invisible Man* in some fairly obvious ways
even if it is the made-for-TV version and, therefore, a commodity
in some important spheres.

But young Greg Morris had been in a couple of epi-
sodes as had been young Bruce Dern, who always struck me as
one of those lower-class white boys who grew up with young
lower-class black boys—gangstas, proto-gangstas—and became,
essentially, one very black dude, "Bruce, my nigga." Both played
various characters in various episodes and in these (and perhaps
especially in those in which lanky, cool Greg Morris figured, under-
playing his roles, tossing off his lines and tossing his shoulders into
a fine young arrogance in those days before *Mission Impossible*) the
show achieved a level of complexity that fronted on a dense incom-
prehensibility—the gobbet was so thick with overlays, it was *invis-
ible*, man! The show had moved ahead as a dark wave of insinua-
tion—try to find the real storm, good luck—on a predictable old

weather map for years, trailing technicians, metronomes, bawds of euphony, TV weathermen in its wake. Or pushing them ahead of it, whichever.

Trains occur with some frequency in both C & W—the true ethnic music of many white Americans—and in the blues and some spirituals as well. "The Midnight Special," "So Lonesome I Could Cry." Two older Jewish doo-wop songwriters recently baffled Terry Gross with their repeated references to "Caucasian melodies": they'd laugh and laugh at their broad thing and she just sat there at WHYY in Philadelphia not getting it. She's not on in my town, though, until six p.m. In the long morning it's time to hunker down to the TV set, check out the leaping blue light. If you look carefully into the train wreck in each *Fugitive* intro you can see that the coaches, tilted and off the track, do not have anything familiar painted on their sides—"Pennsylvania Railroad," say, or "Chesapeake & Ohio," pre-Amtrak carriers of the '60s. They say "Chemin de Fer," God knows where the footage is from. We are far from home my brothers. Anyway, the train didn't take the curve too well and Fate articulates its huge hand and the music comes on up again and again and again and again.

NATURAL ABILITIES AND
NATURAL WRITING

Comatose, lecherous, bored, not aching for a little titillation but not averse to it either: TV nation, 1999. But by spring the official business of impeachment was over and the heavy-duty, philosophical commentators were telling the watchers that "We're all breathing a sigh of relief." Moving on, shaking hands, saluting Bill Rehnquist, toting up the US dollars spent on the whole thing but the money was gone, it was over, though jokes about the money persisted through the summer—it maintained that kind of literary half-life before fading away with the fall.

But while it was going on it was interesting because it was us (a term I dislike, us), big broad U.S. culture having an experience together; tempting to term it—the experience—sexual, but it was more sexually *tinged* than directly pleasurable. It was more a metaphor for sex than sex itself, an itchy blanket under which fucking was more possible than it was a fact (to borrow an image from Nicholson Baker). Perhaps I found it interesting because it *was* representational, because it demanded of Americans—even unimaginative Republican-types—a metaphoric virtuosity that's quite foreign to our everyday national character. We're a technological bunch—from a tradition of tinkerers, Ellison said. But metaphors? Of particular note is that the impeachment made it possible to look at the perpetrators themselves, the Republicans, in terms of theirs. This isn't about sex, said the Grand Old Poobahs. Well it was, certainly, even a moron could see that; but then again it wasn't. Neither of course was it about the stuff the Republicans said it was about—honesty, the Constitution, the law, Clinton as a bad role model for the youth of America; but in the *New York Times* Maureen Dowd said, They want payback, the Republicans, and not just for Watergate, they want payback for *Woodstock*. All those bodies in the sun and the rain caught on film in that movie, often naked, writhing to Jimi Hendrix and Carlos Santana and other jungle music or jungle-inspired music, mostly white kids shaking that thing. Payback for *that*.

(I went to the Goose Lake International Music Festival, Jackson, Michigan—near the prison—the summer after Woodstock, July 1970, nineteen years old, one of the few black kids there. It's a mixed memory: I went with a friend and freely and happily admit to doing the sorts of things one does at a three-day outdoor party but finally, I think, there were too many bodies present for me—naked, clothed, it doesn't matter, groups don't do it. I met a cute little blonde hippie at breakfast the morning of the second day, someone who'd come in a van, who said he palled around with a black guy his age who was over there still asleep right now. "He got a goat and I got a goat too," he said, pulling at his wispy chin. "Late at night 'round the fire we both wolfmen." Wolfmen.)

Tall Vernon Jordan, the soul of black eloquence and haughty post-black grace—both—striding around Washington, a "super-law-yer" by all estimates, a man who moves with "alarming" ease into all manner of campfires, all sorts of powerful situations. One of the southern Republicans, however, thought it ought to be necessary to actually watch Vernon Jordan testify about the whole mess. I paraphrase but the nouns and verbs are correct—he wanted to look Vernon Jordan in the eye and hear his tone of voice and, *that way*, know whether or not he was lying. I recall it being the moronic and endlessly expounding Lindsey Graham who said that, but it was "really" Bill McCollum, from Florida (my mistake occur-ring, I suppose, because of the shared white southern accent and Representative Graham's repeating TV presence), who wanted to look old Vernon in the eye. "You a lie," we said as children, "you a lie." A terrible curse but a beautiful one as well.

Now tall Vernon Jordan, he's a super-lawyer. And trials are, to a large extent, theater—the experience of presentation—and because of that I'd certainly think that Vernon Jordan or any lawyer worth a damn could look you in the eye and lie to you with a song in his heart and an honest smile on his face. But Vernon's a colored boy, and we have that complex, knotty history with white southerners and by "complex" and "knotty" I mean that there's real familiarity—commonality—there and a savage presumption there as well. We are our bodies, the blackness of our bodies is our curse, our cross: his body gon' tell on him, said Bill McCollum, his body gonna betray him and we'll see that he's a liar, that he a lie.

Betty Currie, the other black body at the periphery of the scandal? She was "loyal," went all the descriptions of her, loyal.

In the city in which I used to live—Ithaca, NY—there was a feature that ran on Saturdays in the *Ithaca Journal*, something sponsored by the local SPCA and encouraging readers to "adopt" animals: each Saturday there was an article about a particular animal, a profile as it were, and each of these was accompanied by a clear, crisp head-and-shoulders photo of the animal in question. My ex-wife Katharine Wright is a photographer and also knows a great deal—through various employments and schooling and deep interest—about animals. The photos, she told me, are not to the point: they're being photographed like humans are and animals are much more their bodies—the stretch of those—than we are. In our faces lives our intelligence and our faces are subject to that and malleable because of it: in my family we pride ourselves on being able to tell tall tales with straight faces—a collie shortage in Scotland, e.g., or a forty-foot glass statue of a pigeon at the State Office Building campus in Albany, NY—and we're not even lawyers. I realized some years ago how much physical attraction depends on the intelligence observed, over time, in someone's face. Erica Hunt mentions, as example of double exceptionalism, "the black man who yields feeling cerebrally." Coco Chanel said that by the time you're fifty you have the face you deserve.

Now for a colored boy such as myself who appreciates the outdoors—trees, mountains, hills, the prairie, animals, etc.—this is troublesome when it comes to the natural. Or this is the way we're brought to the natural, *as* the natural. Nature is quantity, its own surface and opaque and mysterious and threatening and, obviously, erotic because of all that, but knowable via certain conventions, discernible, readable—Vernon Jordan's dark body will tell on him, will undo him, will reveal him. Our words don't mean—it's our bodies that mean, that's where our nature is. And because of this we have no particular agency there, in the depiction of nature—our bodies are "primitive" and "jungle" and therefore we are not other enough from the natural world to be able to find metaphors of ourselves there. Instead, we *are* the natural world, we're ripe: upon us can be projected metaphors by nature writers or writers about human nature. Channel surfing late at night I recently got to Zalman King's *Delta of Venus*, the shock of nudity on TV, soft-core porn on the IFC: I watched for a while and then I fell asleep though not before the scene in an after-hours club—there was a frenzied crowded dance in which women lost their tops and their breasts came out and this was called "jungle" in the voice-over. They acted like Negroes. This is old news but on it goes. But it's old news, an easy example.

(But channel surfing again some nights later I came into the middle of *Howling III*, a werewolf movie set in Australia that's too racially weird to even begin to talk about. This was not of course on the Independent Film Channel but on TNT or USA or some other cable channel that panders to our indelicate appetites. But I was struck by a scene in which a white ballerina went lupine in the middle of her frenzied dance—hairy, gray, and savage, she came after her fellow dancers with a hungry aplomb. Same scene as in *Delta*.)

Frenzied sex and nature and us. All this is trouble to me too because I came to understand malleability and provisional definitions and choice and projection all at a long early point in my own life. Nothing particularly mysterious here: reading and thinking and meeting smart people. (Many of whom were ambivalent priests and even more ambivalent religious brothers, the lot that educated me in high school, this being a benefit of the black middle class dodging the bad public schools and sending its children downtown to be taught by the Catholics.) Anyway, when I got to college and read

Blake's hellish proverb about "Where man is not, nature is barren," I
knew that already. I learned how to watch movies by watching mov-
ies on TV with my mother—"Look," she'd say, "look what they're
making that woman do." I became aware that writing and photogra-
phy and movie making and walking in the woods and commenting
on what one saw were not natural abilities or occurrences but a series
of choices, determined in extent by the circumstances of one's birth,
people you've happened to meet and other lucky or unlucky acci-
dents visited on one's person—and this alone, this awareness which
I can't lose when I think or write, would probably be grounds for
my lifetime exclusion from the canon of nature writing.

That canon's even more profoundly white than others. But Eddy
Harris did make it into the *Oxford Book of Nature Writing*, with a
snippet of his *Mississippi Solo*, the book about his canoe trip down
that river from Minnesota to the Gulf. I recall hearing him inter-
viewed on the radio in 1989 or 1990 and realizing that he was black
before the interviewer's questions revealed it—a familiar inflection
in the voice betrayed it to me. I was on a mission to the grocer's but
I put that on hold and sat in the dark parking lot listening to Eddy
Harris on the car radio and thought I could do that, I could write
about unconventional backcountry travel, publish a book about it.
And then I went into the supermarket to shop for dinner feeling
quite odd about having just granted myself that permission. I was
forty years old, a professor, middle class—my Volvo sat waiting
for me in the lot. I'd published poetry books, done the state some
service, and won literary awards. And I certainly understood by
then—had understood long before then—that there was no unprob-
lematic center, that all was margin and—more—that straddling the
margin, like I'd been doing in my writing and my life, was exhila-
rating, the long ride, the dance of flirtation with various kinds of
otherness, with various forms. I knew before I heard Eddy Harris
on the radio that the margin was a powerful place to be, that you
weren't "trapped" there—if you were middle class—and that you
could, because you were marginal (and middle class), do anything.

Surely I talked in my classes about the lack of certain narratives for black writers and women writers but I'd thought I was immune, post-all that.

I bought *Mississippi Solo* and marched through it—it's OK, it's a good read. It did not inspire my prose book *Into and Out of Dislocation*, which is about backcountry travel in Canada, among other things. (It's really a book about ambivalence and about family-as-metaphor, and about race—that is, blackness—and history in the northern reaches of the continent.) Neither the book's content nor its form offer any particular homage to Eddy Harris, but the fact of *Mississippi Solo's* existence helped me be arrogant enough to push my own book as book. The classic path/desire of wanting someone there before you was at work here, even for a writer such as myself, one who's sneered so often at narrative's straight, dull line and at the cliché of role model. But there I was, driving home from the supermarket with food I would cook and, a few years later, there I was out having lunch at a lovely seafood restaurant near Union Square with my editor at Farrar, Straus & Giroux, appreciative—both times—of that narrative and humbled some by that appreciation, by my own realization of the narrative's power.

Of course I remember "discovering" Jean Toomer's *Cane* when I was a sophomore at university and what a powerful moment that was for me; I read it the same year I went to Goose Lake—the music festival was a mixed experience, as I said above, but nothing good or bad about it was particularly unnerving. Toomer's complex blackness married to issues of migration and sex and to his book's own unwieldiness as a book, on the other hand, unnerved me a great deal. My book *Here*, begun 15 years after I read *Cane* for the first time, is a belated response—an homage, really—to it.

But is all this "nature writing"? Or what's this got to do with nature writing, which is what I'd intended for the theme of the theme of this paper to be? I spoke last year—1998—at St. Mark's, invited there along with a hundred other people to talk about "identity and invention." I began by saying, "All my life I've depended on geography, acknowledged it and considered it as basic meaning, as that which is in the world and irreducible in the world." There's nature, right there, boys. But on I went to talk about my invented identity as filmgoer, movies being an art form I truly love in a goofy, romantic sort of way, and to document the film that had most scared me as a child—it was not a proto-intellectual choice like *Repulsion* or *M*, it was a wolfman movie, *Curse of the Werewolf*, with young Oliver Reed in the title role. My piece was short, less than a thousand words as per the instructions from the Poetry Project. Now, a year on, I want to return to that and add some things to it.

I'm interested, simply, in the processes by which people estimate nature, what we bring to descriptions of it, what syntheses. We do synthesize. From the first chapter of Eugene Genovese's book *Roll, Jordan, Roll*: "Slavery bound two people together in bitter antagonism while creating an organic relationship so complex and ambivalent that neither could express the simplest human truth without reference to the other." It's this necessary "reference to the other" race that Genovese suggests that interests me. It's the soul of synthesis, of an everyday self-consciousness that black people *continue* to inhabit. (The relationship is still there, I'd argue, for white people as well, but the *consciousness* of it has burned off or gone underground, choose your metaphor. We still, though, fresh and talking among ourselves, are perpetually, unforgettably other; or, as Dick Gregory said years ago, commenting on the failure of Madison Avenue-type advertising in the ghetto, "We know what it's like to *be* Brand X.") But I was raised middle class and understood and appreciated irony and we were far removed from the "old days," even as I was growing up in the '50s. I was sent to the Nature Program at the Dayton Museum of Natural History in 1958 or 1959, only vaguely aware that I was the only black child present. (My exhibit on Birds of Ohio is boxed in the attic still.) My sister's history is similar.

The question is, Why are the Giscombe children so enamored of werewolves?

If most popular and literary depictions of nature as subject are problematical because they seem to deny—or pretend to deny—human/cultural agency and hypothesize a de-racialized and class-free "human" self whose metaphor might be found in the erotically primitive otherness of the natural world . . . Well, werewolves are an antidote to that, or at least a more direct form of address—we have the human and the animal coupled (not sexually but sexuality enters into it). Popular depictions of lycanthropy are a satire, arguably, of nature writing, a cautionary tale: look too close and you're gonna fall in. (Langston Hughes's "Suicide's Note": "The calm, / Cool face of the river / Asked me for a kiss.") The primitive will inhabit you. This, of course, is what "going native" means, a phrase that only seems to apply, in the customs of usage, to white people. Native? [replacing ME. natyf (OFr. natif) < L. nativus < natus, pp. of nasci, to be born]. If black people are jungly, primitive nature itself, then nature [ME.; OFr.; L. natura < natus, born, produced, pp. of nasci, to be born] will get you and take *over* your ass.

More: the films my sister and I enjoyed so much as children were not the monster films of giant ants or beasts from 20,000 fathoms as much as they were films about human bodies in revolt, infected bodies, bodies at war with their own "selves," the inescapability of the monster's human body—the werewolf in the daytime staring at his hands, the elegant appearance of the vampire in the drawing room in early evening, arguably even the limping mummy, with its human form and memory. What's at stake is the human's inability to truly transcend the heat of its infection, the nature of its nature. Oliver Reed, as Leon the werewolf, was described in a long-ago fan magazine as being in flight "from the curse of his tainted blood"; the language has stayed with me. And blood's a big deal, as a public metaphor for race—it defines black people (in America) as being people with even "one drop" of African "blood" in their veins. It's the one drop that stains you like it would a white tablecloth—it's the thing, the *substance*, that taints you, makes you non-white. This is not news either, this one-drop rule and the fear of hidden miscegenation that it represents for white people. The point I'd argue, though, is that the films we liked constructed their monsters, partly, out of this fear—there was often a heroine to be rescued from some dark sexual beast (Fay Wray and old King Kong, e.g.) or the ostensibly ordinary person is the descendant of some wrong or ur-ancestor as was Simone Simon in *Cat People*, one of the smartest werewolf movies. (Monsters had other Africanisms about their persons as well but this is a topic for another place, another time.)

It's not news but, to me, these old movies were a statement of the fact of miscegenation, because this is what it is, partly, to be black in America—it's to acknowledge the racial mix of your ancestry; to be white, of course, is to deny it. The film that scared me as a child, *Curse of the Werewolf*, came out in 1961 and never entered the public imagination like the first handful of wolfman movies from the '30s and '40s. Prominent among these of course was *The Wolf Man*, which appeared in 1941. The main character, Larry Talbot, played by Lon Chaney, Jr. looked like a normal-enough white guy, but oh what he turned into by night! His hair would kink up and his skin would darken and that big Chaney nose would flatten right out. De woof-man!

(In the most interesting moment in *American Graffiti* one of the minor female characters says her parents won't let her listen to Wolfman Jack—played by himself in the film—"because he's a Negro.")

Real wolves don't look a thing like what Larry Talbot turned into: their fur is very straight, their snouts are aquiline. But he is the werewolf image that has survived in American culture—sixty years on, Lon Chaney's still the wolfman. His depiction made it onto a postage stamp last year, just before the rates went up, the fearsome head printed there next to 32¢. This wolfman as opposed to the metaphorically less complex but higher tech models of the various *Howlings* and the *American Werewolf in London* movies. *The Wolf Man* is from back in the day, and the story itself is simple and cautionary: Larry Talbot, the wayward American son of Sir John Talbot, arrives at the embarrassingly huge family mansion—Talbot

Castle—in England, becomes smitten with a young local woman—played by blonde Evelyn Ankers—who is charming and all (but lower class). He accompanies her and her unfortunate friend—the dark-haired actress Fay Helm—to a gypsy fortune-teller at a traveling carnival. The gypsy—Bela Lugosi in a bit role—happens to be a werewolf and, later that foggy evening, he attacks the dispensable dark woman. Larry Talbot fights the "wolf" off—too late, alas, for poor Fay Helm—but in the process is bitten and becomes, of course, a werewolf himself. The question of the film is whether or not he's going to kill the blonde he's in love with; he does not—he's killed first (by Claude Rains as Sir John) and, in death, reverts to his human form. He's brought back to life for a number of sequels and it's possible, in these, to chart the advances in special effects: in *The Wolf Man*, he changes demurely—that is, off camera—but in later films Chaney's transformations were accomplished in a succession of frames of the same shot: different thicknesses of hair overlay each previous shot until he's finished changing into the dark-skinned, flat-nosed, kinky-furred monster who first went off in pursuit of the English blonde who'd fallen in love with the white boy who came back from America to live in the house that Jack built, y'all.

I saw all these films for the first time at home, when I was eleven or twelve years old, on snowy Channel 9's Shock Theater, Friday nights at 11:30. Years later on the verge of leaving college I saw my first porno film, *The Devil in Miss Jones*, at the Colony Art Theater in Schenectady, NY. I'd seen "dirty" movies in high school but was unaware of how far the genre had progressed. After the first scene, in which Miss Jones (played by Georgina Spelvin) commits suicide, comes the second in which she goes to hell and meets the devil (Harry Reems), on whom she goes down; the woman next to me, my classmate Olivia, kept hissing, "Penis worship, goddamnit!" in my ear but I'll confess to being fascinated watching the actor shed his robe and get hard (the shock of seeing proud flesh, *wood*, in a theater), realizing there in Schenectady that this is what I'd witnessed in *The Wolf Man* years before on TV. Harry Reems indeed. The body changes, grows hair, sprouts a horn, gets blacker, it's all the same. Or similar enough.

Why are the Giscombe children so interested in this? Kathy Giscombe, rolling her eyes at her brother and then getting serious, mentions the spectacle of hidden, angry power unleashed suddenly and unexpectedly. Robert Hayden: "the chronic angers of that house." And this works for me as a both female and black reading of werewolf stories—as well as a tale of the Giscombe manse—but my own interest was always elsewhere. Alongside that but elsewhere. There's a *loup-garou* tradition in Haiti and it's interesting as well but it's also other than this, the depiction of the werewolf as a European-descended American icon, something we watch at the movies or on TV. Alfred Métraux: "A woman werewolf getting ready for a night outing first raises as many fingers as she expects to be hours absent from her house, or else she lights a candle marked with three notches. Unless she is back before the flame reaches the last notch her excursion may go ill. When she has taken these precautions she frees herself of her skin by rubbing her neck, wrists, and ankles with a concoction of magic herbs. She hides her skin in a cool place—in a jar or near a pitcher—so that it will not shrink. Thus, stripped to the quick, the woman werewolf makes movements which have the effect of preparing her for the flight which she will shortly undertake. Flames spurt from her armpits and anus, turkey wings sprout from her back. She takes off through the thatch of her house . . ." In Haiti *loups-garoux* are shape-shifters and devourers of children and the French for werewolf itself fits awkwardly: there are no wolves in Haiti. And the Giscombe children's antecedents are Jamaican and that's a different island. Here in late-twentieth-century America werewolves are nature transformed—*narrated*—infused with the wide human trace in such an ungainly way as to be—as both sight and site—of deep interest or, better, of broad interest. If one's interest is in the dance, werewolves are a good series of steps; they are a *filmed metaphor* perhaps more so than anything else I can easily think of.

More on this: I was on Assateague Island some years ago, the island off the Maryland coast where wild horses still roam. "Wild horse" had always seemed oxymoronic—the term itself a combination of opposites—after seeing horses bridled and saddled, behind fences, for all these years. I was on a several-day cycling tour of Maryland and Delaware with my friend the poet Cory Brown; it was rainy and miserable this particular day but I'd convinced him to go on in that for the extra miles so we might be able to encounter nature in the "person" of these horses. We crossed the bridge onto the island and rode around for a long time on the park roads—I had on a primitive Gore-Tex raincoat but Cory was wearing a green garbage bag and was getting impatient. (The horses of Assateague are descendants of domestic stock kept there by Eastern Shore planters in the seventeenth and eighteenth centuries. "Truly" wild? Well, they live without human agency or without benefit of *direct* human agency anyway—Assateague, which stretches across the state line into Virginia, *is* protected; the Maryland herd is "managed" by the National Parks Service, whose publications suggest that "feral" might be a more appropriate term than "wild"—but the distinction is a fairly fine one.) Anyway, I was anxious to actually see the horses and was not disappointed: suddenly, there at the roadside in front of us, was a group of them, three mares and a stallion, grazing. They're not tall animals, they're stocky and scruffy and shaggy. They're bigger than ponies, though, and the stallion stood still looking at us as the mares crossed the road and disappeared into the brush. This was a harem, I realized, and then I wondered, "Should we be afraid?" He was brown and white, his big penis hung down toward the ground; he snorted at us a few more times before following the mares off out of our sight. "OK," said Cory Brown, "we've seen the fucking horses. Now can we leave?"

We went back the way we'd come, over the bridge to the mainland, and it was on the bridge that I realized that in *The Wolf Man*, people claimed, on the screen, to be seeing a wolf, to have seen a wolf—*Canis lupus*—and *not* Lon Chaney in black face and fur. I remembered the screen image of the attack on poor Fay Helm—it was a wolf (or a dog actor portraying a wolf) that was savaging her kicking form there in the fog, underneath a tree. The gypsy's mother—Maria Ouspenskaya—explained it to Talbot later with, "The wolf was Bela and Bela was the wolf"; but when Bela was the wolf, the wolf looked a lot different than when Larry Talbot was the wolf. And I realized that the figure of the wolfman—clothed, broad featured, hairy, dark, and upright—was a construct for the movie audience, that in the "reality" of the film that figure does not exist. It was a *literal* filmed metaphor, I realized as we chugged up the slick road; it was an awkward fit on the Maryland two-lane and it's still an awkward fit on the way back from the story of the wild horses of Assateague—it doesn't particularly connect or hold together but it's a true story, my friends. The location of my epiphany. We pushed our way through a heavier rain to the condos and high-rise tourist lodgings of Ocean City and arrived drenched and grubby and a little desperate but still managed to fight with a desk clerk and get the price of a room in his hotel down. We watched a PBS program on Robert Mugabe and went out for a wonderful seafood dinner. The ocean's right there, of course; fish tastes different in seaside towns. It's a rainy Sunday afternoon in central Pennsylvania as I keyboard this and I'm thinking of the *loups-garoux* of Haiti: no wolves there so their presence is an act of language rather than an act of God or the devil: it's an act "against nature," an act of opening the field rather than an act of connection.

My mother had dozed through one of the later wolfman movies, the one in which a gypsy girl fell in love with cursed Larry Talbot and then tried to kill him, as a service, with a silver bullet. I explained the plot twists to her the next morning in what I imagine now was likely tiresome detail. But then I pointed out that a werewolf could only be killed by a silver bullet "fired by the hand of one who loves him." This, I realized, was heavy. (This is probably why the Republicans failed to eliminate Bill Clinton: they didn't come to assassinate him with love in their hearts.) "But what," she replied, "if a strange werewolf came to town and no one knew him well enough to love him?"

What's the nature of nature writing? It ain't language, the jagged peaks of sentences, the dewy dells of short paragraphs. Nor is it about "reducing something to voodoo," as Barry Lopez snorted in the werewolf chapter of his book about wolves. Henry Louis Gates suggested that Ralph Ellison was signifying on the titles of Richard Wright's books *Black Boy* and *Native Son* with his own *Invisible Man.* Boy: son: man. Music should come up right about here. Denied the oppositeness of nature, I propose my own iconography: that from the standard "Nature Boy," the road leads crookedly to the wolfman.

IN THE WAY

"Every once in a while I dream about an area east of town that doesn't exist."
—anonymous respondent in Kansas Dreams Collection Project, 2001.

I dream of places so often that the dreams are unremarkable as genre—they vary from one another and surprise me sometimes but that they incorporate or refer to places (or to historical events) is a given. More interesting to me here is the dream I had on the morning of 7 August 2001, a dream of maps in a book—displayed, printed, the institution of authority. They were maps of British Columbia—I know much of the geography there, having crossed the province many times via various means of surface transport. There were three maps—topographical, of three regions—laid out on a single page of a large book, an atlas of some sort: two across the bottom of the page, one on top next to which was text. I took black Magic Markers and registered, on each map, my own progress over the depicted/described/coded landscape. And woke laughing—realizing this was a way of responding to the given, of talking back to form.

"I know much of the geography there"? Better to say it so: I'm *familiar* with the geography. (Since 1991 I've worked at a number of writing projects having to do with my kinsman John R. Giscome, the nineteenth-century Jamaican miner and explorer for whom some British Columbia geography is named; this has included a Fulbright half year in Prince George, "B.C.'s Northern Capital," where the stench of the local pulp mill was understood to be "the smell of money.") The difference is important, the statement of *knowledge* implying a cavalier attitude bristling with the certainty

of connection, an attitude I'm unwilling to take or claim. More to
the point is Nathaniel Mackey's assertion that the "truths" that occur
or appear in a text are partial truths and what's interesting is what's
not there, the presence of which itself persists in the text—if text
is defined widely enough to include its range of implications and
suggestions and connotations—or alongside it. "Poetic language,"
he writes, "is language owning up to being an orphan to its tenu-
ous kinship with the things it ostensibly refers to." I'm quoting his
"Sound and Sentiment, Sound and Symbol," an essay about black
music but which ranges outward from that or around it, and he
reminds his readers, two-thirds of the way through, of an idea in
the writing of both Ralph Ellison and Charles Olson. Ellison: "[T]
he mind that has conceived a plan of living must never lose sight of
the chaos against which that plan was conceived," this from near the
close of *Invisible Man*. And Olson, from "Human Universe": "The
trouble has been, that a man stays so astonished he can triumph over
his own incoherence, he settles for that, crows over it, and goes at a
day again happy he at least makes a little sense."

Direction is a given or so it would seem. Directions are a gift. I
give them, you give them, she gives them. They have a value aside
from cash or from a cash-like value. They're the gift of description
and are infused with the multiple. They're the *figure* I would pro-
pose for a vernacular geography. A seriously mixed text, directions
float over both ground and the map itself. They have the tenuous
relation to both: to the conventional or produced—i.e., worked for,
agreed upon—wisdom of the text of map and to the facts of the
ground. Directions—because of their performative nature, because
of their gift status—are abstracted from all that. In opposition to
that given, "direction" (that slave to vector), is the journey outward,
the one that itself becomes multiple, the one that does not anticipate
closure or that recognizes that closure is at best arbitrary (the end of
the road, e.g., or the bottom of a page). Theodore Roethke, argu-
ably, called poetry "the long journey out of the self": when we lived
in England, in Oxford, I went downtown on our first day in town

and, seeking the comfort of a familiar location, if a literary one, in a
strange land, picked up the Faber & Faber edition of his *Collected*,
and flipped it open randomly and came to that line, my eye lighting
on it as they say. This is anecdote, a story on me and my reading
my situation. I have, I warned Soren Larsen when we began this, a
poet's solipsism. But I'll go on and say that such journeys exist in
some complex relation—more and less than kinship—to the idea
of directions. They—directions—both contradict and incorporate.
Roethke goes on:

> In the long journey out of the self,
> There are many detours, washed-out interrupted raw places
> Where the shale slides dangerously
> And the back wheels hang almost over the edge
> At the sudden veering, the moment of turning.
> [. . .]
> —Or the path narrowing,
> Winding upward toward the stream with its sharp stones,
> The upland of alder and birchtrees,
> Through the swamp alive with quicksand,
> The way blocked at last by a fallen fir-tree,
> The thickets darkening,
> The ravines ugly.

The locations are metaphoric but this is the *territory* of directions—
which way and what'll happen there. "[T]he moment of turning" is
a tad more obvious now than it was forty years ago but there's always
much that's awkwardly over the top in a big work and this is from
Roethke's last book, the one no one memorizes. Important is that
"interrupted" and that the way, finally, gets blocked by something in
the way. This happens and this is the example of how directions con-
tradict the grander sense of conventional direction, of proceeding
unfailingly toward something, as it were, be that something nirvana
or "merely" Kansas City and the crazy little women there. Outward's

necessarily not a vector but the paltry reference to a starting point which may or may not be forgotten—"forget you," black children curse—or jettisoned on the journey, though it certainly enough informed the origin.

Incorporating directions into a journey, even a conventional one, is obvious: they can clarify and "flesh out" what's already on the map—they're the "local color" details that can reassure the traveler about the relation of the typically yellow Magic Marker'd-in route on a paper map festooned with advertising given one by one's hotel in a strange city. I suppose I find contradiction—the trouble one can get into in the city by accepting and following directions from strangers on the street—to be more interesting. But in thinking about any journey one must obviously consider the source—what's being departed from or, in the vernacular, what's the subject position of the departee? How far from your own description or designation are you willing to go? Can you transcend it? How do you throw yourself at trying to transcend it? Another dream of British Columbia: I was driving out from the mountains that are visible from the central part of the province, this in a movie in the dream. I was driving but also I was watching myself on-screen in the theater in which I was the only patron—a white actor played me, though his skin was darkened for the role. Thus separation—or, to the point here, the rejection of certainty (not one *or* the other but both)—is my token of the notion of the journey out of the self: the vestiges of the self are certainly maintained and referred to but what's *not* particularly of the self or central to the self is also met and butted up against. Other presences enter the text, diverting it (or at least commenting on its progress).

But sometimes your designation will catch up with you on the road. I mean that I have to say that travel has always been a trouble for black Americans: I mean that emphatically and there's no qualification called for in regard to either "travel" or "always." A woman I met in San Francisco recently told me how little she liked *Invisible Man*, how much she rejected its metaphoric title because,

"Wherever I go, you know, they *see* me." (This at the "Expanding the Repertoire" symposium at New College—"difficult" black writers including Will Alexander, Wanda Coleman, myself, Erica Hunt, Nathaniel Mackey, Mark McMorris, Harryette Mullen, Julie Patton, and Lorenzo Thomas. We talked at microphones. I don't know the name of the woman I met who didn't care for Ralph Ellison, she was in the audience, but I think Ellison would have liked her—I was yammering about metaphysics, the peril of being reprinted, and the construction of identity in *Invisible Man* when she jumped up and decked my erudition, knocked my cute little Ivy League self colder than a well-digger's posterior.) My mother still makes us sandwiches when we're getting ready to leave the Giscombe home-place in Ohio and return to this house in Pennsy, "so you won't have to stop on the road." A few years ago, my daughter and I did drive from central British Columbia to New York State, a real trip as opposed to the cinematic drive I dreamed long ago, one bearing no real resemblance to the other. We stopped in Seattle to visit friends but then made a point of swinging *back* up into Canada for the trip across the west, this specifically to avoid Montana and its cowboys and Aryans. We dropped down, finally, into North Dakota where we heeded the directions of local informants to a place called the OK Motel in a town called Steele and there entered a *night* of trouble: much screaming, the local police, and finally a midnight flight over the high plains, down deserted I-90. Madeline was nine and quite brave and I was glad that I was there to talk to her about this first real encounter in her life with wild-eyed racism. We dodged Montana all right but they sure caught up with us in Steele. The directions we got in Bismarck changed the focus of our trip (getting from Prince George to Ithaca) into something else. Six years later it's a set piece, a "funny" family story she and I tell; I'll not tell it here.

2.

Vernacular's from the Latin, *vernaculus*, "belonging to home-born slaves," and differs necessarily from the High Church (the literary, e.g., or the Latin nomenclature); and vernacular's site-specific, peculiar to the practice or the place. Vernacular geography then is improvised *local* talk that engages that outward (and that coincides or can with the tame dog of conventional travel as well). But I want to focus on the vernacular here—in the often unexpected situation of giving directions—as being a literal gift, a literal act or process of *giving*. Directions is a gift that slaves—property themselves—can give. This is conversation, vernacular speech, about geography and it differs importantly from commerce in geography, the industry in maps. I buy the Rand McNally Road Atlas at the local Barnes & Noble (State College's only new book bookstore) and I buy the USGS topo maps at Appalachian Outdoors on South Allen Street, near College Avenue; I buy maps of individual states and provinces at gas stations. You can get free maps of counties or pieces of counties from real estate offices but they give these out as part of their larger, big-ticket business of selling houses and acreage. MapQuest, the internet service, provides both maps and blow-by-blow descriptions of the most direct route from one address to another—but MapQuest's website will link you to ways to spend your money at Denny's restaurants and the Fairfield Inn motel chain and the site, useful as it is, is supported by subscriptions from corporations. We—those of us with Internet connections—get to use it as a collateral benefit of that primary relationship, the one based on the give and take of money. Directions-as-gift contain no option for reciprocity and, of course, no twofold or threefold gain for the giver, which is the way of business, being instead neither product nor service (as was always the first question on the old *What's My Line?* game show) but a dance done by an amateur, an improvisation full of gesture and mimed strutting, an evocation of intersecting ways unseen. Directions are a gift but not an occasion for gift exchange (as is said of Christmas and office parties): you ask for them and I give them with the expectation of nothing in return, this also a kind of outwardness. (Or almost nothing—the receiver of the gift

will usually restate it, changing the literal sound some, a kind of
call and response, an improvisation for two voices. "Mah tongue is
in mah friend's mouf," wrote Zora Neale Hurston.) There is a base
usefulness to the gift: it enables you to get from Natchez to Mobile
or Memphis to St. Joe but then it gets personal, specific or peculiar
to both the giver and the receiver, as the best gifts are. (Or see Lewis
Hyde's book, *The Gift*; he wrote, "It is because gift exchange is an
erotic form that so many gifts must be refused.")

When I was on a cycling trip in the mid-1980s I stopped in
Altamont, NY to ask about how to get to Quaker Street; a woman
directed me to "turn left when you get to a big, stinky farm—
my farm!" And last year I took my students to New York, to the
Nuyorican Poets Café in Alphabet City or, I should say, we all went
together. MapQuest got us good and lost in our Penn State van in
northern New Jersey—we crept through streets and neighborhoods
that looked nothing like the lay of the land around State College and
the population on the sidewalks was much darker than the one we
see sauntering down College Avenue and much less clean-cut than
the frat boys visible through the big windows at the new Hooters.
We stared at the MapQuest printout and we stared at the Rand
McNally Road Atlas and finally we pulled up to a convenience store
to ask how to find Hoboken. I asked Kate W— to accompany me
so we could both hear the directions but she said No, that New York
(and implicitly North Jersey) was full of scary people. Serious. Kate,
bold taker-down of male textual nonsense? Kate, the fiercely smart
poetic voyager? Blue-eyed Kate from western Pennsylvania. I pulled
her in with me and the big woman at the cash register said turn *here*
and *here* and *here* to Hoboken, calling Kate "Honey" twenty times,
probably more.

That's conventional travel, that story with its sweet, pretty end.
But within it's the *articulation* that I'd always be touching the cloth
of. The ambiguity light is *on*, articulation being the talking *gift* and
the *talking* gift *and* the breakdown as well into description of nav-
igation and landscape, both. All. I asked Kate to come in with me

because I'm very bad at remembering directions when I hear them. Similarly, I cannot recall the moves in "Flamenco Sketches" or lines from the poems in Ken Irby's *Call Steps*—the most active, most alive things are often beyond the Giscombe powers of recall.

We were going to the Nuyorican (or, in the short run, to Hoboken to park the van in one of the famous Hoboken parking structures and then take a PATH train into the city) but directions on a wide trip, one with no destination or an arbitrary destination, are interesting because they have the potential to change the trip, to give it a new theme or a new line of development. I said above that such directions will contradict a journey—perhaps *divert* is a better word and perhaps *complicate* is best. (The order here's the order of thought.) Heeding such directions makes the traveler aware of happenstance: someone else's agenda—the comparison to a band jamming is obvious—is allowed into his journey and the journey will incorporate that (or fail to after trying it out for a bit). Heeding such directions accentuates the tenuous connection that life has to the map; they prevent you from seeming to triumph over the incoherence of the grand trip—they're a paper order (like a paper tiger) and because of that they focus your view half on the chaos. I met a Lawrence, Kansas man last summer, Ted Fleming; he and I are both bicycle commuters and he said over dinner at the Free State that bicycle lanes sucker you into thinking that you're safe. You better keep your eye on the road.

3.

"A nomadic poetics needs mindfulness," wrote Pierre Joris. Nomadism's handmaiden is certainly directions—if nomadism "answers to a relation that possession cannot satisfy" (and it does) then the statement and re-statement of directions is the *talk* of that relation. By "talk of that relation" I don't mean reference to it, I mean the relation speaking. What Mackey said: "Poetic language is language owning up to being an orphan to its tenuous kinship with the things it ostensibly refers to." It's in the process of owning up to the articulated relation, then, that's when the language gets poetic. You can go this way, Kate honey, but you don't have to—you can decline the gift. *Directions* is the *open set* of relation, more or less infinite in its implications—speech-reliant, variably beautiful, often "undependable." And item 3 from Joris's *Nomad Manifesto*: "language others itself always again —> nomadic writing is always 'the practice of outside'; writing as nomadic practice—on the move from one other to another other."

And the poet Barry McKinnon, in conversation in Cottonwood Park in Prince George: "When you're here you're nothing."

So I'm interested in how the spoken fact of directions creates a bridge—even a "wrong" or "impossible" one, an incoherent one—between a nothing here and somewhere else that's different, an other, a not-here. A jazzy map has its missteps in it—part of the map of the text—and these get transformed by the travelers' restatement of them both as words at first and then as literal actions across a field: I'll play it, a little tentatively, and then you can play it back, this vs. Frank Sinatra's boast of having done it or had it "My Way," the orchestra swelling behind the last line.

Imagination? It's possible and tempting to talk about the clever and unusual ways different populations have of measuring and stating, of describing landscape. I've heard some and more have been suggested to me. But I'm less interested in local verbal custom and the necessary relation that has to product (the barter in imaginative quaint speech) than I am in the actual process or practice of making a tenuous and demanding *way* appear in the air—such a way's made awkwardly out of references and body language, out of speech. In such directions much swirls.

On the California Zephyr, two days out of San Francisco / Emeryville heading east, the woman walking through the coach in a caravan of women and children saying, "I done learned this train like it's my house; I be telling people 'not that way' . . ." Black and white women and children—the group having formed as the train crept toward Chicago, the group free of men. Novels by black men tend to be about white people and novels by black women tend to be about black people. The "not that way" comment's not symbolism's clang but token of the references to the world of the train (this world / this train), that and the commitment to the multiple, even as—or especially as—the multiple becomes chaotic. (This of course being one of the points of *Invisible Man*, to be able to live with one's head "in the lion's mouth"; another is the novel's commitment to the transformative nature—or *power*—of speech.)

My current big prose project is called, for now, "The Traveling Public," the book-in-progress about trains and train travel and all the metaphor that goes with all that. I'm interested in the relation of poetry, railroads and geography—this is not directions and the gift of directions, this is something a little bit beyond it or behind it. Traveling between central Pennsylvania and California one changes trains in Chicago and the layover's long so you can range over downtown and through the Loop and still get back to Union Station in plenty of time. The vision I had was when I was going to go in through the wrong entrance for Amtrak, the one on Madison Street that only leads to some Metra platforms, to just those commuter trains—it's all business down there, just the blunt rears of the fluted-steel double-decker cars and they're grimy and dirty and present as well are the railroad smells of diesel fuel and human piss and mysterious grease. I realized my mistake halfway down the stairs— that this was not a way into beautifully refurbished Union Station with its Art Deco lettering and its marble, its skylights. Realized my mistake but saw that I was looking at articulation itself, the unpretty but very movable warning-striped back ends of those cars. Thought more or less immediately of the beginning of Nathaniel Mackey's "Ghede Poem":

They call me Ghede. The butts
of "angels" brush my lips.

The soiled asses of "angels"
        touch my lips, I
kiss the gap of their having
                gone . . .
Ghede, the loa at the doorway, the figure of death and Eros at once;
and Kamau Brathwaite describes Xango or Shango thus—"Pan
African god of thunder, lightning, electricity and its energy, sound
systems, the locomotive engine and its music. . ." But that's the
Islands and the Giscombes left there last century for *this* and to ride
these trains here, not to be ridden but to observe and comment on
the ways toward elsewhere. To deal with the rocky road, to scheme
on the favor of what's in the way. But on those stairs in Chicago,
"player with railroads," what was shown to me was how some of
that distance is stated—here I mean the literal *difference* between
Chicago and Berwyn or Chicago and Naperville or Chicago and
Winnetka, the same kind of difference they talk about in math. This
was the navigation I was looking at, this was navigation's body. All
those stations are lovely—American cathedrals to the idea of travel,
goes the usual idea about train depots—but the travel itself is that
fluted steel, that piss smell.

Music at the close: I came, on Amtrak, from central PA to Kansas
City where Soren Larsen picked me up. Just like in the song that
Wilbert Harrison sang:

        Might take a train,
        might take a plane,
        but if I have to walk
        I'm gonna get there just the same:
        I'm going to Kansas City,
        Kansas City, here I come.

The song shifts at some incontestable yet nearly invisible point on the way: the singer turns from the set of his home companions (including, implicitly, "that woman," of whom—should he stay with her—he will die) and addresses the chaos and opportunity of K.C., this by addressing the city itself. I'm no longer going to Kansas City but coming. The shift's the articulation, the shift's the way.

BRICK MAGAZINE INTERVIEW
(WITH FORREST GANDER)

FG: *Giscome Road* begins with song—"The song's a commotion rising"—and your prosody is remarkably musical. Sometimes the poem seems to be a musical track for which "forms descend / & bend away & cross over / (not returning much to the theme)." Did you conceive of the whole book-length poem in terms of any overriding (operatic? a canon? symphonic?) musical structure?

CSG: How pleased I am that you noted the music in the poem/ project; this feels to me like a good place to begin. But I certainly don't know enough about music to use it as a basis for composition. I've actually always found myself a little outside of music—I mean it's inconceivable to me how anyone could actually *write* the stuff. Listening the other evening to Pharoah Sanders, though, and—later that same night—listening to Miles Davis's *Sketches of Spain* and *Kind of Blue*—once again those guys helped me see the possibility of music. I saw (and of course *heard*) Miles Davis only one time, at the Kool Jazz Festival in Saratoga in 1985: one thing I remember is watching him step in—as though from some sort of outside that existed right there on the stage—and impose a very temporary order from time to time on the band's playing. I don't recall who was in the band or even most of what they played. But I recall noting that evening that his aloofness was different than that of Wynton Marsalis, who had played earlier—Marsalis would also step in with that order but his order was about proficiency and an impermeable edge and Miles Davis's stepping in was about range. Miles Davis's order was, as I recall it this evening thirteen years later, an escalation of whatever the band was doing and a comment on what they were doing—I mean it was almost a tease, he was always a little ahead of them, a little unpredictable. He was a shape, out in front, across a line.

And the other thing I recall is watching him stand at the edge of the stage with his back to the audience and play "Human Nature," the song that Michael Jackson made popular. He played it casually, if piercingly; he tossed it off. Yeah, that's human nature, you know us. I make a couple of oblique references to that title in the body of *Giscome Road*. Get a couple of beers into me and I'll say that the whole book's an homage to Miles Davis playing that song that night.

At times, I suppose, I *had* thought of all this writing not as a soundtrack (as I say somewhere in the book's final section) but as the *description* of the soundtrack to a film. A film about what? The north I suppose, Darkest Canada. In a travel essay I wrote some years ago after coming back from two tours of northern Ontario there's a moment of lament about leaving North Bay, the very funky market town on Lake Nipissing: "One needs songs," I wrote, "to sing on the road, of the road—music should have come up, some sort of as yet unimagined straining *northern* jazz, an *insistent* strain, say, of straying muted horns, fragmented, breaking." I normally try to keep the essays and the poetry apart because they serve different purposes—but here they intersect, I think. Or the moment in that essay names something—describes something—that I want poetry to do.

There's much *about* music in *Giscome Road* but it's less an "overriding structure" than it is a series of references; I hope the music manages to name *and* trouble direction.

(Here's an organic bit: Miles Davis died a few days before my first trip to northern British Columbia and as I traveled north that fact and that music traveled with me; I don't think anything about that made it into the book but it affected the way I saw that landscape for the first time: it was kind of a big deal for me—meaning it was an inescapable connection—that in the silence of the north the music in my head was "All Blues." "I'd come up through a long silence on the way," I did write in the book's third section. I've been back up there many times since then and I still can't be on very silent Upper Fraser Road and not hear Miles Davis.)

FG: You make references in *Giscome Road* to the writing of the poem, so that in part the poem is a record of its own construction. At the same time, you are tracing a blood line, a railroad line, a poetic line, and determining the coordinates of a particular place. At one point, you write, "I had a taste for ambiguity / & arrival." By crossing the various thematic lines of the poem, you induce a taste for ambiguity and arrival in the reader too. Yet isn't *Giscome Road* less a book of arrival than of approaches, of tracings and edges?

CSG: I realized during a reading tour a couple of years ago how much I talk about edge. Maybe it's out of that that I'm now commencing a book about the Midwest, announcing early that it, Illinois, is edgeless—for the acknowledging link with the previous work—and then going on. It feels very weird to quote myself but I found this in an earlier book, my 1994 book *Here*:

> but memory divides, then itself dogs
> all the shapes at once, the dense edges of them,
> the empty hearts . . .

Both *Here* and *Giscome Road* are full of references to empty hearts, to the hulking hollow nature of things. Heart / source / core identity— all those things are fictions, I'd argue. The edges are what matters; *becoming* is what's important. How's one become? You edge in, you edge on over. One can talk too much of these things.

The heart's empty but the blood's a presence. It's in motion, it's always out there making its rounds. Blood, of course, is quite ambiguous, quite a loaded metaphor. I'm fond of J. A. Rogers's series of books *Sex and Race*; they're documentations of miscegenation throughout the ages and their particular concern is black-white mixing. Even now in the U.S. the "one-drop rule" is a blood metaphor with social force, it's something to be reckoned with, it's got teeth. Rogers's books—which are remarkably well known in the black community and kept in print by, I think, his daughter—are a documentary refutation of racial "purity"; I was pleased to be able to wedge a quote of his into the book's first section.

I talk a lot about blood in *Giscome Road* but a lot of the talk is ironic or half ironic: I mean we talk, as a miscegenated culture, about blood relatives, about blood being thicker than water. We call each other blood—or did within recent memory—on the street. The Coen Brothers' first movie was *Blood Simple*. And perhaps most important, black people say "Blood will tell." What line or series of lines is it that makes a face black—how does one recognize and surprise blackness in a Caucasian-seeming countenance? (Sherley Anne Williams on a photo of Bessie Smith—"I surprise girlhood in her face.") In one of the more hallucinatory moments in the book I talk about "the countenance of that man's woods." How does landscape look—or sound—black? It's this question that I'm trying to make some noise about in *Giscome Road*.

Giscombe or Giscome is a name West Indians recognize as a Jamaican name. Family mythology names Portland Parish, and Hope Bay and Belcarres—places in northeast Jamaica—as sites of family origin. I've been to Jamaica and will go back and someday write about Jamaica but I say that on faith—I don't know what I'll write or how. The British Columbia landscape, though! The fact that there's this Afro-Caribbean name for the way into the Arctic! Oh this is range.

(A particular place, a point to reach in all that range out there? It was George Bowering who alerted me some years ago to the fact of there being a village of this name in B.C. I found out later that it was named that by the railroad because it was the townsite close to the famous Giscome Portage, the shortcut into the Arctic Watershed "discovered" by J. R. Giscome in 1863. That's a pocket history. There are still some "reachable" Giscome places in northern B.C., places called Giscome in all that range, but once you arrive at one of them you realize how tentative arrival is—there are places that have the name on them but you arrive there and then go on.)

FG: You take obvious delight in the fact that there's an Arctic route through Canada with an Afro-Caribbean name which also happens to be related to your own name. "What range!" you say. But it's a range you continually describe as centerless. And just as the place the speaker is searching for has no center—"There's no center where / similarity would begin," so he "came to necessarily centerless space"—the speaker of the poem is himself described as "an outline," a tracery around a missing center. Is he also searching for his own "dark heart," as though he were, at the outset of the poem, emotionally empty ("at the jagged rind / of the empty / old heart"). Aren't we given to feel that among the discoveries the poem makes, there is a very personal one too, involving the speaker's own being?

CSG: Nope. I've tried to keep that part out of the book. The point is—in terms of the human "center" or lack thereof—that we went up there (we meaning black folks) but we didn't stay. There's an irony there, it's funny. I take my headnotes seriously as part of the poem: the cover's a picture of McDame's Landing, named after John R. Giscome's partner, the Bahamian miner Henry McDame. McDame's nothing but a place-name now, the same's true for Giscome. "The name's the last thing to disappear," I say, which is a revision of the J. A. Rogers quote on Bolivar's African ancestry that comes a few pages later: "This portrait of the great liberator painted in 1810 shows, in my opinion, a trace of Negroid strain in the fullness of the lips, usually the last trace of Negro ancestry to disappear."

The speaker's own being? Being's edge, it's the push outward. A friend who owns a successful bookstore suggested to me once that someday he'd be wealthy but that he'd always have to work really hard. The speaker's being's like that—you gotta be active or you're nothing. There is no heart, edge is all; and I mean edge also as a verb. It's out of that idea that I list all those nothing hearts in the one "Northern Road" moment—

a heart as tho' it were hidden down in the rocks, a faceless heart

a creole heart to say the unhidden gaps in all edges up & down
the road

(a heart that hammers & swings, both)

a damned soul, a plateau

This is also of course one of the nods to the tradition and Sterling
Brown. I've yakked up above, of course, about edges.

Two things, one looking back and the other looking on: first the
cover photo of McDame's Landing (taken from across the Dease
River) which I found on the British Columbia Archives web site.
I was struck by its quite coincidental resemblance to the Robert S.
Duncanson painting, "View of Cincinnati," that's on the cover of
my book *Here*. Both are landscapes, both feature a river and build-
ings across that river just up from its shore; and, in both, the settle-
ment—the city of Cincinnati or the Hudson's Bay post, McDame—
is framed by hazy hills that merge with an ambiguous sky. Nobody
did skies better than Duncanson. And of course each landscape has
a black edge to it, something unbeknownst to the casual observer—
Duncanson's blackness still surprises people and though McDame's
the name of several locations in B.C. and is often referred to as
a place marker, you still have to dig pretty far down to get to an
account that tells you (a) that there ever was anyone named Henry
McDame and (b) that he was black. (Oddly enough, once you get
down to a place that identifies the name as having been attached to
a real guy, at that level he's always "Henry McDame, a well-known
negro miner" or some such description.)

And second, looking on. I feel like I've documented empty heart
syndrome in this book and in the book before this book and I'm
tired of it. Edge, edge, edge. When I say, up above, that the new
book's about edgelessness, this is part of what I mean. The Midwest

is of course the heartland and good God! what a cliché that one is. But that's where I'm trying to go now, in the new work. I think I'm writing a trilogy, as insufferable as that sounds—the *Here* book, the *Giscome Road* book and now this new, barely started book which is some prosy lyrics "about" the stuff of Illinois, about "feeling evil," about being evil there in the heartland.

But that's future. In this *Giscome Road* book, what's the speaker looking for since it sure ain't the heart? Some sort of black thing, amorphous yet total, an edge that permeates, a tincture that makes landscape itself black, a countenance of that man's woods. Something that'd *permit* the speaker into the landscape, some kind of possibility. You never know how the blood's gonna appear.

FG: You say the music is less an "overriding structure" than a series of references that name and trouble direction. This fascinates me. We notice, of course, that throughout *Giscome Road*, the speaker orients himself by a road that parallels the river. The river and road are each connected to histories the speaker learns to read. But the speaker is also listening to a "long song," "a commotion w/out words." These three interweaving and metaphorical currents—river, road, and song—suggest to me the "songlines" by which Australian aborigines maintain their land and memorialize their own cultural history. Is that particular notion of "songline" one of the master metaphors of *Giscome Road*?

CSG: Don't know enough about the songlines to comment on them, certainly not enough for them to be a "master metaphor"; someday I'll read the Bruce Chatwin book, start with that. I love the bark paintings and Nicolas Roeg's movie but I'm a westerner (or as James Baldwin most correctly said, "a bastard of the west") and, therefore, a tourist in all that, at least so far. Your question, though, made me mindful—because of its identification of river, road, and song—of one of the early dreams I had of the north: the road into the north paralleling both river and railroad (a true enough and common industrial archetype) and the smaller road that splits off from that road, crosses the tracks and then Ts, paralleling the "main" road but invisible from it (existing behind a line of scrub or bushes), the secondary road being lined with the houses of poets.

The three items are broader things for me, things past the peculiarities of my dream life; they're African-American archetypes—road, river, railroad. The title of the book is—or was—a conscious restatement of the title of Sterling Brown's first book, *Southern Road*, and within my book are nods to him. There were more ostentatious nods at various places in various versions of the book but you know how revision goes. The point is that his book's title *permitted* mine.

PHILLY TALKS 18

Public conversation between C. S. Giscombe and Barry McKinnon.

(From C. S. Giscombe)

Barry—Finally some notes for you. Rereading *The Centre*—in the context, perhaps, of *In the Millennium* and "It cant / be said"—I'm struck by how the book plunges at the close with "Arrythmia." As though the rest of the book were a jam leading up to it. The earlier sections are easier to read—they're more airy (meaning ventilated, as it were, by speech and space both) and both lead up and don't lead up to the final section. Plunge? One thinks of bus plunges, a staple for some years of *NY Times* reportage about Mexico—they went over those cliffs all the time, according to the *NY Times*. Shuddering downward—one imagines—rather than being airborne, a plunge full of ambiguity and in necessary stages, complex and articulated. Not always fatal but fatality was always part of the story. The book quickens there, at "Arrythmia," in "Arrythmia," and—forgive the pun—slows at the same time: the question of mortality has been raised and the answer is complicated, thick, more open-ended than the rest of the book, more subject to provisional statement that is itself of course full of question. E.g.:

> caught in a Saturday afternoon, slight hangover
> work done - sex ahead, beer, steak - the mystery of wife from her
> complexity - yielded simply to the admission of love?

And it's that the book is full of speculation and observation, "Thoughts/Sketches," and improvisations against a background—the

64

articulation against that or within it of a center and what a center (as we spell it in down here in the States) might contain or travel with. But you trouble that (which I mean as praise), you trouble the background (meaning the first two-thirds of the book) for "Arrythmia" by saying, in that final section:

> . . . believe it. but on the path – to feel as abandoned
> as the woods, still & silent knowing the silence of the higher
> force.
> dog, his head in the snow.
>
> believed. go on – it is all made like a bed board, cut and sim-
> ple. it is
> a name like February – dark, to blue, dark to light, not as
> backdrop.

These lines are fairly terrifying and anticipate the two long poems you handed me in New York last summer, *In the Millennium* and "It cant / be said." (Reading *The Centre* this morning also, oddly enough, in the context of one of the train books you passed me, along with the poems, that day at St. Marks; anyway, I'm realizing as I type this that both of those quotes above impact, more or less, on my experience of *The Canadian Pacific in the West*. I'll bring it up later in a way that I'll hope will not be too cloying.)

In the Millennium defines the world, right on page one, as "a contradiction of attempts at connection to it" and that gets restated on the next page as "diminished in the global sense / so much caring becomes diminishment"; later this mutates again—"my aging / exaggerated // by the fight against it." This ain't no happy poem but it documents the now, as it were, of the future. In the poem the thing—including the future—finds a mobile truth in its opposite: the world's defined that way on that first page.

Perhaps this is the moment (or "the instant") to mention something you said to me when we were walking (summer 1999?) in

Cottonwood Park and talking about the future itself, retirement, etc., and the relation to geography. "When you're here," you said, "you're nothing." Not meaning Prince George in particular but then, all meaning is local. I was impressed enough of course to remember it and to want to apply it to this work in particular, which I see as a way—because of those self-cancelling oppositions—of documenting the instant; or, more to the point, the poem gestures at the instant even though—or because—it's not here. It's nothing; it's here *and* it's nothing at the same time. (It's a similar thing, obviously, to what we got to the first time we met in 1991. I was on my way to Giscome, B.C. the next day and it was a place that you had been to and—maybe important for this context—you'd videotaped the town's destruction, that the lumber company bulldozed the houses—company-owned—after pulling out and resettling the populace. Anyway I was going out there for the first time and we agreed—this after some beers—that it was there, that there was a there there, that Giscome was a place even though there was nothing there. OK, this is the sort of thing I see you doing in this poem and in "Arrythmia" as well. I set out that next day for Giscome with that opposition very much in my mind and it feels as important to me today, reading these poems, as it did that evening ten years ago.)

In the Millennium's the place beyond the end of the roads, the place where nothing is. It's different from the cleverness, say, of Mel Lyman's title, *Mirror at the End of the Road* (though Lyman's book, though romantic, was interestingly ragged and almost unreadable in places); it's where the poem goes, on out into the nothingness. All comes, as you say about the late valentine flowers, to zero, even with "bonus points" added. Here's the millennium. And yet the poem's furiously local: you allude to snowmobiles (which can deliver us quickly to the future) and "in lifes regret" becomes, in the following line, "downtown in slush."

It cant / be said? Well, no, it can't. I suppose I see this as a continuation of the nothingness I see documented in the previous poem. And of the contradiction—it can't be said so write to say that. What emerges in both is the peculiar emptiness there is to big events: that the language—and its images—doesn't match the thing. This I take to be the topic here, that failure. Death? Well, that takes place in language too, doesn't it? (I don't want to get going talking about death but I have to say, to remember, that when it became clear that my friend Marianne Marsh's husband was going to die from his cancer I went in to speak to her about that and she just sighed and looked out her window and said, "Yeah, we've got a lot of shit to deal with." The same language would apply to buying or selling a house, to being on a contentious township committee, to planning for or cleaning up after a big party.) The world's blank canvas is out there: throw some death at it and that's just bonus points still adding up to zero—the impossible dichotomy between the resolved and the unresolved. You say, "There's no subject but time that contains our demise."

Impossible for me to read this poem and not think of Baldwin's *Notes of a Native Son* (which I taught quite recently, just a couple of weeks ago). The essay's an account of his father's death and also an account of the racism that Baldwin himself encountered working in defense plants—this was during World War II—in New Jersey and the racism that black soldiers were dealing with. "The tensions" (as newspapers call it) erupted into a riot in Harlem, this in August of 1943. Baldwin wrote:

> . . . On the morning of the third of August, we drove my father to the graveyard through a wilderness of smashed plate glass.
>
> The day of my father's funeral had also been my nineteenth birthday. As we drove him to the graveyard, the spoils of injustice, anarchy, discontent, and hatred were all around us. It seemed to me that God himself had devised, to mark my father's end, the most sustained and brutally dissonant of codas. And it seemed to me, too, that the violence which rose all above us as my father left the world had been devised as a corrective for the pride of his eldest son. I had declined to believe in that

apocalypse which had been central to my father's vision; very well, life seemed to be saying, here is something that will certainly pass for an apocalypse until the real thing comes along. I had inclined to be contemptuous of my father for the conditions of his life, for the conditions of our lives. When his life had ended I began to wonder about that life and also, in a new way, to be apprehensive about my own.

But the odd point that I'd wish to make in regard to this essay, Baldwin's, is that the account of the death of his father and his account of racism and riot don't entirely connect. Instead, they coincide. And they lay out certain things but the essay's not tied up neatly. The local apocalypse is coincidental to the father's death and I think this is fairly important. The essay jars and jolts, which is what good writing does.

* * *

In New York, you were kind enough to give me a couple of train books that were your father's (your uncle's?), knowing of my fondness for trains and railroads. Fondness? It's an old attachment, full of metaphors having to do with sex and memories and observations having to do with race (I'm old enough to remember the Jim Crow waiting rooms in the stations in Birmingham). And, as Alan Gilbert has suggested to me, there's a centerless quality to the North American railway system that I find important as extensive fact and reference.

I'll go on briefly about one photograph in D. M. Bain and D. R. Phillips's book, *Canadian Pacific in the West*. (And I'll try to figure out how to scan the photo in and ship it to you later.) It's Eric Grubb's photograph of the track ahead, taken from the brakeman's position (the left side) on the cab of a steam locomotive, when the train was stopped alongside the Ottertail Siding a few miles west of Field, B.C. The photographer was leaning out the window and visible in the picture are the latch for the window itself and the long curve of the locomotive's boiler; the siding is presented joining the single-track main line and the Kicking Horse River and Tocher Ridge and, in the gray distance, the President Range take up the majority of the photograph's surface. The train is evidently stopped in anticipation of a "meet" with another train, one that would be coming from the opposite direction. "When it was decided to include the photograph in this work"—note Bain and Phillips— "we had no data about the train and the meet and it was decided that the caption would be prepared with information that can be surmised from the shot." A lot can be surmised: location obviously but then there are no white flags flying from the front end so it's not an "extra" train but a scheduled one. It's possible to tell that the switch—via which the siding joins the main—has already been thrown to accommodate the oncoming train's movement onto that track. Other things as well. One thinks necessarily of Pound's translation of Li Po and his commentary:

"The Jewel Stairs' Grievance"

The jewelled steps are already quite white with dew,
It is so late that the dew soaks my gauze stockings,
And I let down the crystal curtain
And watch the moon through the clear autumn.

NOTE: Jewel stairs, therefore a palace. Grievance, therefore there is something to complain of. Gauze stockings, therefore a court lady, not a servant who complains. Clear autumn, therefore he has no excuse on account of the weather. Also she has come early, for the dew has not merely whitened the stairs, but has soaked her stockings. The poem is especially prized because she utters no direct reproach.

But of interest to me is that the picture (quite alone in this volume which contains twenty-three photographs) defies the photographic genre of train porno. Train pictures tend to be "wedge shots," the head-like engine of the train coming at you at an angle so that you can see both the engine's side and its front end; the rest of the train streams out behind the engine, diminishing in size. Imagine a sperm cell. In Eric Grubb's photograph, the train's a set of machine details and these suggest the *potential* the train has to get itself down the track; this rather than the conventional and common picture of the train actually doing it. Grubb's photograph documents Eros, the *place* of desire, not the depiction of desire itself, acted out.

I had lunch at a pleasant restaurant—The Sidetrack—in Field in summer 1997. I'd been cycling with friends from Jasper, down the Icefields Parkway to Lake Louise, and we'd split up there and I was a little sad on my way, the first all-day ride alone, from Lake Louise to Golden. But what's in the journal is this, about the place I camped in Golden: "A few minutes ago was the moment I like best for viewing the mountains: the sky's a pale blue without illumination, a static blue and the snowy mountains are static too in their whiteness before it." I'd thought at first that the mountains in Grubb's photo were the ones I wrote about but the direction's wrong—the range in the picture is near Lake Louise, not Golden, this in spite of my breathlessness at having "recognized" them. But it's the color value that survives in my memory and is similar to what I see in the picture. That and the starkness. Cycling, the mountains (and the prairie) are not scenery—they're places to cross, to soldier through; they're not scenery—that's for people in cars. You said, "dark, to blue, dark to light, not as backdrop."

A fondness for railroads? Well, the world's geography; I mean geography's irreducible in the world, a fact, opaque. Railroads describe it.

—C.

(From Barry McKinnon)

cecil: a few weeks ago on the phone I asked: what are we going to do? - a question regarding the why, when, what and where of the philly talks. we both began to laugh/ nervously. but this to say, you've plunged ahead and given me a wonderful essay/letter, new poems and notes I'll respond to here - make a plunge that I hope gets me to somewhere and you - to connect our journeying / returns
    into the large concerns of our talks: poetry & . . .

the complex practice of it that we may stand reaffirmed / ashamed together, also in a kind of happiness and laughter - bound as we are to attempt its secret/lead our lives by it - baffled dumb/ to want/ any need to journey / return.

ten years ago: you in normal illinois and me in prince george, b.c. - an unlikely geographical connection, your voice on the phone - smooth, subdued, quiet, intelligent and polite beyond what I'm used to, introducing yourself quickly, a poet/a project - and to make a simple request: you needed an invitation and a letter to support your plan to track the black explorer and miner john robert giscome's journey and life in the mid 1800s viz his presence in b.c., on your serious premise of a family blood tie.

j.r. giscome / c.s. giscombe

and within a year, there you were in the parking lot of the down-towner motel in prince george. did I wave first or did we wave simultaneously? (we gave no physical clues for identification. I knew from scant historical information that j.r. giscome was black/ you couldn't be white (I'd have been very suspicious if you were!)

the   blood ties.

now, here, your return via john giscome to begin the long journey
- almost a decade ahead of you - into the poem:

giscome road

our immediate connection / spontaneous

difficult talk/easy talk. we, familiar with similar materials or lack of
them, and questions - and a sense of a share in a cursed journey, if it
were not for the almost promise that its very activity is what could
equally save anyone on it.

we talked

into the night. back porch beer epiphanies/ and over the years of
our talks to a kind of necessary knowledge - as if by articulating a
shared skill, concern, and practice, each step ahead be taken more
assuredly - give simultaneous courage in the foolish prompt to risk

                    words

        the wilderness   the nothing

dumbly /   head out

as early miners packing each thing for a journey into vast unknowns,
up the physical canyons, thru miles of bush I can barely walk a block
thru (cecil, that day on the giscome trail in the sheer and wonderful
context of the "historical" moment, being with you, I was also being
bled by many species of carnivorous bugs - and in fear noted trees
shredded by recent hungry bears. how far did we go until we got
the idea: this, now, here, the literal giscome trail/ his portage on
to summit lake/the water

shed divide at 54 40 - longitudes and latitudes of history. I watched you swim out   quite a way.

our subject? what tools, what corporeal/ mind/ necessity let us start with an agreement, spit out without a thought, yet a thought we continuously return to by virtue of its curiosity - to a "theme" of sorts: "this is a place we decided, but there's nothing here."
right   and   wrong

the name's the last thing to disappear

giscome/giscombe no more saturday nights there. who cares in the expectation of dislocation as normal in the canadian northern corporate practice and ethos? in recent history (the 50s) the cheslatta indians "removed" from their land by the alcan/kemano project, given scant hours notice before the flood. giscome emptied on scant notice in 70, (there's a long list of other towns and people) - and most recently tumbler ridge, where I write this (a coal mining town shutting down) - a place in a huge transition that very much attracts me. in its disintegration to become a ghost town for eco tourists, old age pensioners, snowmobilers, poets, and misfits - I begin to feel, illusionary or not, a sense of being, temporarily, out of dislocation: these beautiful mountains, and air and cheap real estate - a real place in the detritus after they've gone, whoever they are (innocent or not). I'm thinking of the what&who in the ruthless discard of primal economy. what of value can be kept?   what's changed in america, the north -

here

& giscome, the town in 71, where joy and I felt not at home, but that this place was a home; she photographed each house, street, the school, the train station, mill, the machinery and every thing abandoned.

on one of those trips I drove out along eaglet lake until I feared
going on. this sense of nothing ahead. a road to end without
reason. where would I be in this momentary terror - my soul I lit-
erally sensed, gone - cast from the earth into the diffuse centerless
light. is this the dislocation, or the terrified connection - (poem,
now, as portage of our own necessity and making - words as map,
tendril, trail and path to return to where? the poet going forward/
back on a syntactical bridge only strong enough, in this necessity
- because we're travelling light - to carry only his/her own weight?
the words/words

got   you   to giscome road.

no back drop
.

here

you made words/large fact of a world once blank, almost empty,
almost nothing/ went back ward for/word into terrestrial multi-
ples: jamaica to the babbling old man/ - a long lost giscom(b)e on
a front porch - knew nothing you needed to know: no evidence at
the primary source: therefore
.

cecil giscombe on a ten speed, poet pedaling into the centerless
light: jamaica, north america, normal, prince george, giscome, the
prairie midwest - into

diffuse light.
                (feet, head, and eye

into -

nowhere/somewhere, far, two directions, with open return. into
& out of . . .

describing fit

                           head out
endnote:
many of the thoughts in my improvisation bounce from cecil's title
into and out of dislocation. I think I'm just beginning to understand
it (beyond the medical description of cecil's injured/ dislocated arm
as described in his book) - in terms of his life and writing as an afri-
can american writer in america, and canada. the title poses a great
millennial question: if we know, with varying degrees of intensity
the arbitrariness of what being into dislocation is, (aren't we all in
it, or about to be?) - then what is it to be out of dislocation? the
place this question imagines is open to what human values we would
presently wish to define it as (a real place without compromise or
illusion?). what presence & location do humans anywhere have in
the current psycho/sociology of what has happened/happening here/
anywhere you care to look? (the world's largest clear cut in the bow-
ron valley, is 40 minutes from prince george - large, invisible; it's
"nothing," they say. the unrecorded world, this close, (20 minutes
from giscome) - yet, minimal fact given the human dislocations
& disturbance of the larger daily world eco/human diaspora. a
question:

the task of poetry?

poetry/

what I've wanted. the poem itself (an artifact/ real place) - & have

I also wanted the very moments of its act & its energy (integra-
tion/location) - to include, as well, a necessary, disintegration of its
conscious and unconscious premises? by this I mean the practice I
think I see in george stanley's new work: he writes / builds a line
that seems dismantled at the same time - to reveal accurate processes
of mind and life moving to their jagged truths. this want of a new
world! this want of the new poem! get a life, I hear them say while
"real life goes on" into and out of the language and world at hand.
into & out of . . .

I think the task - & cecil so large among the others I admire for
taking it on - is to break form, break ground, be ground (not back
drop), so that when the radio's on, the static clears.
now voice and music are heard, and the pleasure of the information
to make what need be known and said, visible.

works cited:

the line " journeying and returns" is the title of a book by bp nichol.
the line "reaffirmed/ashamed" is from william carlos williams's poem
proclaiming: "I am a poet! I am a poet!" references to "this is a
place, we decided . . ." is from cecil's essay "border towns, border
talk" published in *diverse landscapes: re-reading place across cultures
in contemporary canadian writing*, (prince george: unbc press, 1996.
beeler & horn, eds.). "the name's the last . . ." is from *giscome road*
(normal il: dalkey archive press, 1998). various titles I've taken from
prairie style, cecil's ms. in progress, "real life goes on" is a robert cree-
ley quote on the back jacket of *into and out of dislocation*.

Barry McKinnon
tumbler ridge/prince george
jan 2001.

(From C. S. Giscombe)

Barry—A quick final note before we buckle down for the trip to Calgary. It was your concern with Giscome, B.C., by the way—and Joy's photographs of the place in *Repository* magazine—that got me up into all this business in the first place. George Bowering saw the pix (and mentions them in your interview with him in *Open Letter*) and, years after, when I was corresponding with him about other stuff, he recalled them and the name of the town in question and suggested the coincidence to me.

I'd intended—as I said on the 'phone last night—to include an outtake here from my talk on innovation and miscegenation (which touches on things Fred Wah talks about in his hybridity book which just came from Amazon.com) but this afternoon, even edited, it feels too bulky, fibrous. Maybe we'll get to it in Calgary.

Tried to fold in a scan of the marvelously erotic train photo I mention in my previous note to you but the equipment has failed. I'll Xerox copies and pass 'em out next month.

* * *

words

the wilderness   the nothing

An ABC on nothing here, in continuing response:

A. That being here's the statement of or about being static (or the static itself), unmoving, a sitting duck, an easy target. Nothing. That it's quantifiably better to keep moving and, as Mr. Paige's conventional advice goes, not look back. In movement's trace is something affirmative: movement's a statement of ability, of will & process.

From Pierre Joris's *Nomad Manifesto*:

1) that language has always to do with the *other*, in fact, for the writer (l'écrivant) is the other.

2) that there is no single other, there are only a multitude of them—plurality; even multitudes of different multitudes—hetero-pluralities.

3) language others itself always again—> nomadic writing is always "the practice of outside"; writing as nomadic practice— on the move from one other to another other.

B. Alongside that is that one can make the nothing palpable. When I began writing about the Midwest I had a vision (?) of the voice speaking from nowhere. And so, at the risk of sounding romantic, there's the desire—in speaking from nowhere—to articulate the nothing. Here, I think, our intentions coincide some: you said, "we, familiar with similar materials or lack of them, and questions - and a sense of a share in a cursed journey, if it were not for the almost promise that its very activity is what could equally save anyone on it."

C. So we talk.

—C.

RESPONSES

Wayde Compton:

When I read C. S. Giscombe's *Into and Out of Dislocation* I came across his rendering of an African-Americanism: "no matter where you go, no matter how far, no matter to what unlikely extreme, no matter what country, continent, ice floe, or island you land on, you will find someone else black already there" (10). This aphorism is familiar to me, but not through a black channel, through a Chinese-Canadian friend who once told me something basically the same, with an addition that, if grafted to Giscombe's, would read like this: "no matter where you go, no matter how far, no matter to what unlikely extreme, no matter what country, continent, ice floe, or island you land on, you will find a Chinese family already there, and they will be running the restaurant." Jeet Kei further added that this family you will find will probably have no history or background in restauranteering, but will have quickly figured out that by virtue of being Chinese alone, people will buy their food, and will "buy" them as restauranteers. Jeet Kei told me this because I had just come back from Inverness, Scotland and was marveling at how strange it was for me to be in a town that was mostly white, but more than that, a place where the white people were all of the same ethnicity. My friends from Inverness, when I talked to them about the seeming racial homogeneity of their town, explained with some pride that there was now a Chinese family here. Yes, they ran a restaurant. In Thomas King's novel *Medicine River* the Native-Canadian protagonist receives a letter from his brother who is wandering abroad:

> "Dear Will," [the letter said] "Thought I'd write to let you know I'm still alive. Didn't get to Australia yet. Stopped off here in New Zealand. It's a real nice country. Hey, it even has Indians, but they call them Maoris down here. I'm taking off for the South Island tomorrow. Going to climb a glacier. How are you doing?" (144–45)

There is always someone _____-_____ already there. No matter what continent, ice floe, or island you are from, you will find someone also from there too, where'er you roam.

I wonder if this aphorism on farflung-ness is a lament, phrased as Giscombe has heard it in that particularly African-American way of dryly expecting the worst. Why would someone black preceding you be negative? Because I also wonder if the aphorism isn't meant as a cautionary proverb: there is no escape. It's akin to the saying, "The only two things you have to do in this life are stay black and die"; there will be no remove to individuality, there will already be the images and tensions of your race wherever you get yourself stranded, so don't get any ideas about getting away from it. If you are James Baldwin in a secluded Alpine village surrounded by French children clamoring to touch your kinky hair, claiming to have never seen a Negro, dig a little deeper—you'll find that there were blacks in that very village in the previous century or millennium, bootblacking or conquering from elephant-back. The people there—the people wherever—are always going to believe they already know what you are. The aphorism is cautionary.

Ishmael Reed, on the back-cover blurb for *Into and Out of Dislocation*, says it "reads like a modern slave narrative, only the writer, a university professor, is seeking heritage instead of freedom." But Giscombe is not dogged north for simple connection to ancestors who preceded him, but rather it's an inversion of Afrocentrism that moves him, an Afroperipherism, an Afrocentrifugalism tugging him to the outskirts to find a cipher who himself didn't fit the description, to the place where identity may or may not cohere. John Robert Giscome was not a runaway slave, was not exactly a hero, was only maybe a direct ancestor, who went to the edge of things and stayed there, who didn't complete anybody's idea of an odyssey, really. But his name got affixed to the ground not unlike a vèvè. Names on the ground are more tenuous than Roots.

In American Giscombe's imagination, I realize, I am the "someone else black already there." I am, against all the lessons of my life here, somebody's autochthon. Wow. Although I was born here, my work has been a long seeking for precedents and a slow coming to belief in this place as the actual place of my ethnic making. Joe Fortes is my Vancouverite "someone else black already there," though I have not traveled to here from elsewhere. Imagine the words "born in the outside" sung to the tune of "Born Under a Bad Sign."

"There are no black people in B.C." is a commonly voiced rhetorical statement, and what it says under its breath is, ". . . and the exceptions you can trot out don't count because they're not real blacks." We have B.C. ancestors—the blacks of the nineteenth century—but they are, like Nathaniel Mackey's remythologized Andoumboulou, a population who did not reify, who failed to multiply or stay, and who were, all said, not really the progenitors of the black population that is here now. In Wilson Harris's novel *Jonestown*, the narrator, obsessed with the unexplained abandonment of certain Mayan cities before Columbus, writes:

> I dreamt I had been robbed of my native roots and heritage. I suffered from a void of memory. I belonged to peoples of the Void . . . But there was a catch, a shock of breath, in this sensation . . . The shock of the "peopling of the Void," the animals of the Void, the creatures of the Void, became so extraordinary that "extinction" imbued me with breath-lines and responsibilities I would not otherwise have encompassed. I became an original apparition in my wanderings . . . (7)

So extinction allows for reinvention, so what? It's all still blues.

Is Giscombe's black travelogue a quest for Shklovskian defamiliarization, a way of making "black" strange, to make it either over there or back there, to look at it again, to look at self again? This is a different kind of yearning than Jack Spicer's deference to "the outside." Spicer's "Martians" and "spooks" (he called them that sometimes, yes) were an expression of a desire for remote control that only one more or less already in the driver's seat could intone. But, O my I.D., I feel like a porter's son; I'd like to drive for a change. I don't need any more of the outside in me; outsiders done staked enough cantons in me already. I think Giscombe's "out there" is different, is a blurring crossfade, not a Spicerian disavowal. There's a mutuality he expects, and that's different than a romantic jettisoning of ego in the woods.

So much of the African-American subcultural imperialism we

suffer brings us "black" as tough, redeemed, definite. "Say It Loud
(I'm Black and I'm Proud)" therefore I am. Brian Fawcett writes
of Malcolm Lowry living "in the interzones between the worn-out
Cartesian universe and the wilderness" (Popatia 77). Giscombe,
cycling, wants the rubber to meet the road on those and other
interzones.

CITED

Giscombe, C. S. *Into and Out of Dislocation*. New York: North Point
    Press, 2000.
Harris, Wilson. *Jonestown*. London: Faber and Faber, 1996.
King, Thomas. Medicine River. Penguin, 1991.
Popatia, Geneffa. "Decoding 'Difference': Using Race Theory to
    Interrupt Nation-Building Discourses of Alterity that Underwrite
    Anthologies of Identity Formation in Canada." Burnaby, B.C.:
    Simon Fraser University M.A. thesis, 1998.

George Elliott Clarke:

Subject: Re: Giscombe/McKinnon
Date: Thu, 25 Jan 2001 10:19:46 -0500

On Thu, 25 Jan 2001, George Clarke wrote:

> I'm sitting down at 11:15 p.m. and trying now
> to respond to the pages [. . .] and I'll register
> again my discomfiture with e-mail [. . .] Here goes!
>

>
> The thematic, the trauma (?), that runs through the
> exchanges last week twixt Giscombe and McKinnon is
> one strikingly, brilliantly, unavoidably too (?), of
> Fear and Terror, as if these states of anguish were
> two jealous Gods. Strange and rich how words like
> "terrifying" and "terror" (as in "love might be a
> terror") strike across the paragraphs of Giscombe
> like Old Testament lightning, and then how "fear"
> and even "terrified" connect McKinnon's own fierce
> replies.
>
> But then, maybe what's going on is a mutual looking
> at the void and the omnipotence of roots, place,
> identity, the SEARCH, which is everything, though
> maybe not likely to end up grounded in anything
> but the grave. Yes, it's one locale that the poets's
> thinkin bout place keeps gravitatin toward. When
> Giscombe comes to McKinnon's Arrythmia, he sees,
> lookin into the abyss of the page, the sense, he
> sees, "Shuddering downward," like an emblem of
> danger and death, image(s) of "bus plunges" in NY
> Times Day of the Dead reportage of Mexico, but
> the point is "the question of mortality," and the
> lyrics—discontinuous, direct—of McKinnon are
> "fairly terrifying" because they recognize, suggest,
> "Death" that it "takes place in language too." The
> downbeat of it all is that the excavation of the site
> of being is ultimately funereal, or a dredging up
> of fossils, of talismans, or simply an unmasking
> of place as gravesite: "the local apocalypse" that
> Giscombe sights in Baldwin's riot-torn Harlem. His
> seeing that all rhetoric is a passage through wilderness

> to nothingness, the wilderness—"terrifying"—of place
> we's all ULTIMATUMLY displaced from (save for the six-
> feet-deep/shallow six-feet-long, 3-feet-wide void
> we do get to "fill"—temporarily).
>
> What is we all but VOICE, a taste of wind, foul, sweet,
> circling, unleashed, ephemeral, except for what gets
> grounded, in electricity, ink, even arranged light
> on some screen, a VOICE that is comin from somewhere,
> someBODY, formed outta memory of accents, traces of
> sayings, hymns, them SPIRITualS, expletives, gasps,
> wailings, stutters (nostalgia), the hot cussin often
> necessary, howls, sighs, hmmm, all of it meltin
> instantly—terrifyingly—like Giscome, B.C., the
> place that's no place save for what Voice poet Giscombe
> come and give it! Voice is the place it's in, the
> "all meaning is"—"furiously local." (Can I get an Amen?)
> See, what we understand is the vanished Giscome, in
> unBritish undeservedly Columbia, is spoken through
> someone's memory and someone's voice, especially if
> raptured, transfigured, in a poem (portable void a
> voice fills). When McKinnon re-member (re-populate)
> that there village/trace, that place "emptied on scant
> notice in 70" becoming, like other desolated places,
> a "ghost town," him people the void with spectres,
> 'hants,' him do what the poet must, give shape to
> the disintegrated, voice to the disappeared, to
> make the wasted lands spring forth with witnessing,
> protesting, re-membered ghosts: so the stones cry out
> and the trees talk back and the slain oppressed rise
> up and put on flesh, make 'er dry bones stroll,
> march, dance right on top the supposed grave!
>

> When McKinnon say "the name's the last thing to
> disappear," think of the absurdity of headstones,
> how, yep, the names be the last thingamajigs to go!
> This kinda stony, imposed "immortality" (in
> memorial marble), of course is unreal as Ozymandias'
> desire, and just as unstable. Quick to self-destruct.
>
> What we may want, even if a-"feared," like McKinnon
> say, "going on. this sense of nothing ahead," even
> the terror of the "terrified connection" that is the
> poem, what we may want is faith in conjure, in
> conjuration of the passed-on, the abandoned, the
> forgotten, the recollection of the voices, the truth
> in the voice like the gold in the mine, to comb dirt
> and detritus, yep, and come up with draughts of gold.
> What Giscombe say, "at the risk of sounding romantic"
> —!!!—"there's the desire . . . to articulate the
> nothing" and the nobody and the nowhere, meaning We
> are, us poets, archaeologists and mediums, historians
> and coroners, paleontologists and priests. IT IS
> unavoidably ROMANTIC! Romanticism be the desire to
> conjure up the speech of the dead souls and the
> devastated animals and greenery.
>
> You see, what McKinnon AND Giscombe is saying, not
> in so many politics-polluted words, but das capitalism
> don't want to hear no rememberin, no histoire, no
> gone—disappeared—anythin, no "obsolete," no "passe,"
> no nothin already consumed and no "consumer" now long
> consumed by worms. Uh uh. De Romantic/Gothic project,
> natchal to des poetes, be to disRUPT dem capitaliars
> by resuscitatin de victims or de resisters, restorin
> 'er voices. De threat of vengeance is de horror dat

> de re-assemblin of de words unleash for de master
> bosses. You hip? Remember! It's the poetized words
> that strike back at evil even after you's dead,
> buried, bones!
>
> Checkin out, checkin into, Giscombe's Inland (sense
> of place resonant in title, think "landin"), you get
> the plot (the space, also the narrative), a foxiness,
> the clarity of the necessarily sly, necessarily
> predatorial, words "coming into view, as if to meet"
> —nay, devour—"the speaker." It's about comin inland,
> settlin, becomin "an image, an appearance in the
> literature" (a foxy deed, that), "a fixture in the
> imagination of someplace," becomin—like aggressive
> pioneer/explorer/conqueror of yore—statuesque, but a
> pliable statue, flexible, maybe even phantasmal, like
> the man says, "a favorite ha'nt." Yo! You, poet, like
> any place, disappear into mere words. You go "Lincoln-
> esque": nothin but skull fragments, stovepipe hat,
> and, most important, Gettysburg Address. You got to
> choose yo remains eloquently. Uh huh!
>
> Then too, I like how Giscombe get certainty next to
> uncertainty: "half a belief's better by far or one
> broken into halves" even though "love's a terror"
> x 3. Then how he autopsies "race relations": "White
> men say cock and black men say dick." Here be some
> definite clarity. And "Eros," like brothers always
> knew, be "tawny," "swarthy," "more 'dusky' than 'sienna.'"
> The colour of an "Afro-Prairie." Amen to that re-
> definition, buffing. For truth is in the vernacular
> like gold is in dem hills. What it comes down to:
> "Any man's body is an open set, a splayed intersection,"
> of course, also, "a little terror." What's the terror?

> O silence, O inarticulation. Why? True damnation is
> having no words, no way to call a poem, a tree, a
> lover, beautiful. But, BUT, buT, Love is "inarticulate
> and lazy." No contradiction, that. Rather, a splendid
> ambivalence: inarticulation=terror=love. You navigate,
> find your way, your balance, no final answer: you understand
> the poetry is not answering any question about music, but
> "(Still fielding the question about music)," i.e., raising
> your VOICE in your PLACE.
>
> Looking at McKinnon, again I see, the focus on "momentary
> terror" and also heavily light ambivalence: "nowhere/somewhere,
> far, two directions, with open return. into & out of . . ."
> Ian Fleming (Bond guy) said, in one of dem novels, "It is
> better to travel safely than to arrive," a somewhat cryptic
> sensibility, but a sense of it exists here, McKinnon
> writing, "in fear noted trees shredded by recent hungry
> bears. how far did we go until we got this idea?" Really,
> in McKinnon too, see a terror of eternity. His essential
> question, Poundian, "what of value can be kept?" Oh my,
> oh my. It's the damned/damning question that only
> eternity can answer. All us would-be Ovids, all us would-be
> exiles from our own time, preferring to lounge in eternal
> glory, we cower before the Judge who will choose: Time.
> —George Elliott Clarke

Looking again at the exchange, later in the same morn, I ain't said a word yet bout my own location, its voice, specificities, its nearness to grave and to oblivion, comfortable, comforting, ya know? So here I be, rattling the bones of the hard-plastic alphabet, in a room in Toronto, English-speaking Canada's "greatest" (in size) city, on the border of the first-tier First World (not necessarily "Free" too), just 90 or so minutes from the true Promised Land (by car), gateway: Buffalo, NY! But the language spewing from off my fingertips—like

sweat or film of DNA'd bio-grease—got formed in skull-womb by
my black/Micmac mother's voice (singing natchally in de African
United Baptist Association de Nouvelle-Ecosse [Nova Scotia] church
[local]: Cornwallis Street United Baptist Church, founded by
escaped slave, Richard Preston, in 1832) and by my father's African-
American mother's/West Indian sire's voice. SHE was James Brown/
True Confessions/Eaton's catalogue/Coca-Cola & boiled pigtails/
Santa Barbara (fave soap opera)/Wilson Pickett/Aretha Franklin/
Rex Harrison/Elliott Ness/Montreal, Quebec/kindergarten/ nice
hats/silk and satin whenever possible/black-eyed beans & rice with
hot curry/rum/children/all dat/voice; HIM was Yma Sumac/motor-
cycle Eastern Seaboard/calypso/ CBC radio/Walter Cronkite TV/
Harry Belafonte/Beatles/ beer & pretzels/carpenter & social work/
locomotive railway (cf. Giscombe) black male wid fedora, scarf,
overcoat stylish/angry and suave/frustrated folk-artist/ voice. Also
influential: ocean, salt smell, Atlantic, spirituals done old-style,
weepy-eyed church vocals, black folk still black amid all dat snow,
a certain rum (rhum in French), Alexander Keith's (pronounced
"Keats" by us "Africadians") India Pale Ale, wimmin toilin in rich
white houses, menfolk layin tar on rooves or scavenging in the city
dump (Africville in Hfx demolished just like Giscome!, sir), sail-
ors (Amurkin or Wessinjun) comin for da gals (too purty, wid da
straight-hotcombed hair, smell of butter and raisin or just fresh-
April'd linen!, kisses full of sultry wine, and dem hips/behinds, good
for da limbo!), 45s and 33s brought up from de "Boston States,"
a whole culture—Negro US—in exile under the British flag for
200 years plus!, world-class nasty pugilists risin up out de alleys of
Halifax, goin toe-to-toe with Ali (in him decline), or rippin into
other world heavyweights, rippin off Olympic medals left and right
(usually silver), or occasional musicians (think Nelson Symonds of
Hammonds Plains, NS, jazz guitarist now resident in Montreal)
jammin wid da Duke hisself in long-gone Africville ("Sophisticated
Lady" got composed for him Nova Scotian-rooted gal pal), or there's
a theologian—Black Baptist of course!—goin from New Glasgow,

NS, to Princeton Theological Institute to teach(!), or some dip-
lomats, federal politicians, ferryin genetics of apple blossoms and
chemistry of molasses off to world-capitals, some of us folks even
migratin to Africa (especially Sierra Leone), or there's rhetoric of
back-country guitar, of bootleg moonshine and a lover's gold or
mahogany or ebon leg, of pressed 'naps,' of woodstoves (Southerly)
and pumpkin pie, fresh mackerel shouted in streets!, smelts in April
jacked by flashlight, of seaweed and seagulls, of some fool wakin
everybody on the Cosby Kid-like city block by blowin taps on his
dented tin bugle every dawn at 6 a.m. cos he'd been in the US
ARMY!, and Bible lessons, you got it, and lemon oil to clean up
ashy legs/arms, and Langston Hughes poems to keep the spirit, and
lotsa British poetry—make it Shelley and Byron and Yeats, s'il-te-
plait—cos it was a UK colony once, and the white gals smilin too
your way (now-and-then), and taste of harmonica out a window,
trains moanin, some delicious tension in yo drawers, some delicious
release too (etc.), and so—Me come from all the above, with a
cracked voice, some British banjo mixed with black-ass piano, some
Canuck mojo, some Nofaskoshan accent, some unplacated place . . .
   —George Elliott Clarke ("Rex States")

giovanni singleton:

This and all along . . . Initial experiential view of Giscombe/
McKinnon . . . coming at it from many directions.

[Note: The "response" following this note has taken cues from
several things, most prevalent among them—my present gig as a
teacher of the endlessly debatable thing called the "Jazz Poem" and
also by recently mandated "Rolling Black-Outs" here in a geographic
province commonly known as "California." The shear irony of the
state-wide "Stage 3 Power Alert" has truly been something to see

and not to mention that whole darn chad business with its resultant 4-year Bush sentencing. And at this moment, I'm hearing prophecy raining down from the Sun Ra Arkestra's "Along Came Ra" as sung by June Tyson:

> When the world was in darkness
> And darkness was ignorance
> Along came Ra (2x) . . .

Luckily for me, sunlight does stream through via the writing of Cecil Giscombe and Barry McKinnon. Within the context of a life being lived, what follows is my spiderwebbish approach to McKinnon's long poem "walking," Giscombe's book Giscome Road, and selections from his long work "Prairie Style." There are also references to other works and topics mentioned in their correspondence. Hopefully, there are sufficient guideposts. Onward.]

* * *

"One day it will happen. It could be happening now that a voice from another dimension will speak to earth. You might as well practice and prepare for it."
—Sun Ra

Looking at or seeing a tree may attune one to one's own bark. Human nature. Try to be natural. What's happening out there in the margins? or in our very own armpits? A drop contains an ocean. Bodies of water. Our bodies—land and water. To know the lay of the land. Ourselves as land masses. Geography of the interior by mapping the exterior. Uncovered/discovered maps as thought patterns/ waves, anatomy of the brain. Repetition.

Exploration where the boundaries dissolve. Observe the one between the comedian's joke and the audience's laughter (if there is any).

To travel. To traverse. "This land is my land. This land is your land
. . ." Giscombe's "Inland" and *Giscome Road*. History, our own and
all of it, is always exactly where it was made, its place of birth. And
what of this music? To make it one's own. Musicality of the forest
and of a bear's heavy steps. Caution. Washed ashore I'm sure. Tell
us what you know. What got you here? Has nature curved back
around and become ours?

* * *

The word "Giscome" yields:
    is
    me
    come
    so
    go

The word "Giscombe" yields the above plus:
    be
    comb
    mob
    gob

Predestination. Turn on "be" and "beingness." Au natural. The sky
too has beat its own path. Stars litter and light it. This being our own
good fortune. A battery for longevity? As if by being there, I could
be there. Maneuvering this is the way it is sometimes. You don't have
to be hooked to have dreams. Hands, feet, forks—all things con-
necting us to down here. McKinnon and Giscombe move us closer
to higher planes by flying us down low. The keys are in the listening.

    When angels speak
    They speak of cosmic waves of sound . . .
    —Sun Ra (from the poem "When Angels Speak")

"Sound Carries" section of the book-length *Giscome Road* pub-
lished by McKinnon's Gorse Press and included in *Giscome Road*
was got to by way of "Imagine the Sound," videotaped interviews
with musicians Cecil Taylor, Archie Shepp, Bill Dixon, and Paul
Bley. Punctuated too by accidental discovery of Bill Moyers's pub-
lic television spectacle *Sounds of Poetry*, featuring Jane Hirshfield,
Mark Doty, and Lucille Clifton. Sound records most relationships
to streams, roads, and meadows. For the record. In *Giscome Road*,
maps and diagrams mutate into mirrors of interiority. A handbook
for trekking over the edge. The edge and the end but not a com-
pletion. Bird Watching may help us remember how to fly. Dolphy's
fluted wings.

Flight. Fleeing. And for trains. To Barry, Cecil wrote:

> Tried to fold in a scan of the marvelously erotic train photo I
> mention in my previous note to you but the equipment has
> failed. I'll Xerox copies and pass 'em out next month.

Writer moved to California from the East Coast on a train so to
see the middle. Flatness. Prairie. Towns and country. Cows and the
Continental Divide. Open space. Traveled this uncovered/discovered
geography via Percival Everett's 1985 novel *Walk Me to the Distance*
set in the "big-sky country known as Wyoming" wherein one char-
acter says to another, "The edge is where you should be, brother!"
And Everett's work is an "edge" typically known as the Midwest and
the West. In his novel *God's Country*, set in 1871, Everett maps a
rewritten Great American Western complete with "criminy jicket"
and "figgered." One main character is a Black man named "Bubba"
who is reputedly the best tracker in the West. Finders. Keepers.

Trains too were a sanctuary for Duke Ellington. He loved the sound of the whistle up ahead. Made for compositions. Trains track. Soundtracks. This A Cool World we living in. Recording of the stretched out lines of writing detail *Giscome Road*. Hobos hitched rides on freights. And too Neal Cassady et al.

Much consideration of the slipperiness of the "center" notion as much as that of the "border." Although I am without McKinnon's *The Centre*, I'm intrigued by Giscombe's note to McKinnon about it:

> Rereading *The Centre*—in the context, perhaps, of In the Millennium and "It cant / be said"—I'm struck by how the book plunges at the close with "Arrythmia."

A plunge that slows. Gets to the end(ing). In the poem "Favorite Haunt" from *Prairie Style*, Giscombe writes:

> . . . I got to be an appearance at the center of things, a common apparition, neither heaven nor hell.

I'm still believing "center" to itself be an "appearance" or is that "apparition." "Arrythmia" as being "neither heaven nor hell." A question of the necessity of borders and of crossing them (up). The primacy of love and loving. Could this be wailing? McKinnon and Giscombe on the nature of love. Both get going and get to the thick of things. Expansive elements. Was it already here upon our arrival? Before our eyes and needing the warm and reassuring (is) comfort of words' expressivity. From McKinnon's "walking":

> are greener pastures over the hill in a storm cloud? in
> scotland I didn't quite know

Eros located in every country and every animal to be sure. Dare we go up to it, greet it and be believed? McKinnon continues:

my own dark self

in time decay- & endless day out to desert/metaphorical sea.
still
to complain water is not the world
to guess at
where the walk will end. near the sea?

It is said that the crawling comes first. Then the walking. But then
we become but for how long? Certain motion is not mysterious.
And mystery clings still at the beginning and ending of each step
taken.

What has the weather to say? In *The Waves*, Virginia Woolf looks
from a train and becomes "part of this speed, this missile hurled at
the city." And later, of course, her body, her breath waves good-bye
and is hurled like a missile at the sea.

I'm now left more curious about the ways/manners in which we
quench our thirsts. John Coltrane's "Sun Ship." Jimmy Garrison
"walks" his bass alone. Call and response for a 5-minute climb. As
we follow a trail or the sun, so too the trajectory of illumination and
its eventual descent into . . . A whistle or bell.

california
01.22.01

MISCEGENATION STUDIES

Report from "Expanding the Repertoire: Continuity and Change in African-American Writing" (Small Press Traffic and New College, San Francisco, April 2000) and Environs.

(Will Alexander, Wanda Coleman, C. S. Giscombe, Erica Hunt, Arnold J. Kemp, Nathaniel Mackey, Mark McMorris, Harryette Mullen, Julie Patton, and Lorenzo Thomas. Called into being by Renee Gladman and giovanni singleton.)

1.
(Paradise Palms Café, University of Hawai'i at Manoa, March 2000)

So difficult here in this, the west beyond the western, the west that's so far west it's eastern, the recently sung-about wild wild west, so difficult here to think the racial out into the categories of home. Home? This island's got its zip codes and its familiar traffic patterns—the old true joke of its Interstate highways—but it is an island beyond the range (past the effortless imprint) of European America: mostly the dark island faces here in the big Paradise Palms, only a smattering of haoles, some Asians, occasional Africans and, if I look extra hard, some African-Americans (a campus cop this morning, two tattoo'd students, a grim guy with a professor look to him) although almost certainly more or fewer than I think, more or fewer than I recognize.

Back on the mainland, family is my metaphor. Back home. Brother, we call ourselves. Sister. Manoa, Honolulu, Hawai'i: Portuguese sausage and two scoops of rice for breakfast here but here in the Paradise Palms the memory is St. Louis last summer, visiting family and Pete—my cousin Pete Samples—and I doing what we do which is cruising bookstores in University City and talking as we cruise. Often it's difficult to accomplish but the necessity, I realized that time last year, is for black people of bookish inclination to *see* one another, to spend time with one another, to be physically present with one another. This is not to take anything from the lifeline of virtual communities and letters via U.S. Mail or Canada Post: those things have their place. But we've been defined and known by others and, significantly, among ourselves as well in terms of our bodies. Including our literal voices—I *recall* hearing Elvis Mitchell's blackness, tricking that out of his voice on NPR, making him as one of us before my white friends at the affiliate station at Normal. Sometimes—in spite of and because of the obvious pleasures of recognition—all that's a curious burden, a strange and shifting load to balance and carry. In the white media we appear as bodies (opaque at best when the medium is most merciful, and more often unreflective, reactive, dull) and yet my desire is for the physical as well, to see both the body and the intellect that animates it—the face rueful, say, or weighing something.

(Normal, Illinois, named for the old state teachers' college, now Illinois State University, my previous employer; but I live now in State College, PA and the new boss is Penn State. University City, Missouri's the St. Louis suburb in which thrives Washington University. Schools define us and reveal us—to borrow language from Ken Irby—or they threaten to. Barnes & Noble stores in all places: the university voices, like the ones on local TV news shows wherever you go, are all the same.)

I came back from Hawai'i with a Bamboo Ridge anthology (a gift from Susan Schultz), *Intersecting Circles*, subtitled *Voices of Hapa Women in Poetry and Prose*, "hapa" being the word for "mixed." This is Miscegenation Studies, or a voice-laden aspect of it, miscegenation itself being the unspeakable, unassailable text, the metaphor (for the dangerous and spoken-of culture beyond the body) that names the body and indicates what bodies do. One of the book's editors, Marie Hara, revises Hughes's old "Negro Artist and the Racial Mountain," saying, "Standing astride the paradox of racial assumptions, we insist on commenting as individuals, not as bridge people or as advocates of any prescribed cultural script." Well and good but the most interesting part of the book comes at the end, the gallery of pictures of contributors. They're not "good" photographs in particular: the familiar studio shot of Jessica Hagedorn is the exception that proves that. The pictures tend to be blurry and too busy both or, more to the point, the faces are too big for the frames. The impulse to metaphor here is simple and deterministic—if the frame's "a racial category" the fact of the "mixed" face itself troubles that—but the pictures remain interesting beyond the impulse. Pictures of the bodies themselves, not the obvious sexualized take but the hands and face and attitude, what Gwendolyn Brooks—writing of corpses—named when she wrote, "Each body has its pose" that "is its and nothing else's." That brings things closer.

2.
Notes for a Talk at *Expanding the Repertoire*
(Essex Hotel lobby, San Francisco, April 2000)

I don't put much stock in "voice"—the consistency of an authentic mask—in poetry but when I break down the constructions of culture, class, etc. there's an opaque thing I get to: the pleasure of voice itself, meaning the vocal (including of course what happens in *singing*), the ironically almost non-verbal *presence* of voice, that kind of physicality.

Harryette Mullen and Wanda Coleman alluded—in previous panels—to the familiar situation: often being the one person of color, the lone black, at social and/or literary events, events which in my case have most often included me because of my relation to one school—that is, university—or another. Most of my fellows on these *Expanding the Repertoire* panels are roughly my age and I imagine that many here have, like myself, undertaken intellectual adventures, have made our bookish forays, mostly among white people—almost thirty years later looking back at my four undergraduate years at SUNY Albany I cannot recall hearing of any black professor, and by the time I'd burned through the ring of lecture classes and had a schedule full of seminars I was almost always the only black student in class, English classes having been for me my first literary events.

And because miscegenation's the fact in almost every black American family, I would argue or suggest that the commonness of miscegenation is a *way* of looking at black literary experience including this inclination toward experiment—that is, I'm agreeing with Harryette Mullen's point of yesterday that being "innovative" is coincident with being "in-between." This is no endorsement of the tragic mulatto business—it's no tragedy to have to think about your origins or your situation. Nor is it a back-turning on blackness in favor of some kind of "mixed" categorization. My understanding is that acknowledging one's mixed heritage is at the root of being black. This is Alex Haley's sly nod from the TV. At the root of whiteness is, apparently, a *denial* of the same thing—whiteness is the claim of purity and insofar as it is that, it's a static position, fixed, desperately hovering.

I've been grateful to Erica Hunt for much and now I'm also grateful to her for her talk yesterday, particularly for her reminder of the importance of a "reading strategy" (that "sometimes finding sources of the avant-garde is not so much about authorial intent as it is a reading strategy, it's the way you read the text of the past"); and she went on to talk about Baldwin—"Reading the past proposes a present sense. I read now and notice that the elegant movements of a James Baldwin essay are not just a function of a deeply engaging subject matter but the masterful manipulation of the tensions of intimate register and public speech to dilate the thought of a sentence, to give the reader a sense of going in, in, in, closer to the 'voice' of consciousness."

But my reading of Baldwin began in the mid-60s in Ohio, under the direction of a priest—Father MacDonald—who taught at my

high school, and Baldwin was the first black writer I read at all seri-
ously. I was aware at sixteen of his *articulation*—but I thought then
that he was just "being articulate," that his level of expression and
difficult clarity was enough, not starting to appreciate until some
years later the cost of that level of clarity, the *active* nature of speech
("something ironic and violent and perpetually understated in Negro
speech") being transformed into writing on a page, appreciating later
still that what I was seeing as I stared at *Notes of a Native Son* was
the *trace* of something very expensive, the evidences of what Erica
named. Voice of consciousness? Baldwin reminded his nephew, in
his famous 1963 letter/essay, "You come from a long line of great
poets, some of the greatest poets since Homer. One of them said,
*The very time I thought I was lost, My dungeon shook and my chains
fell off.*"

And some of the first poetry I witnessed—in the flesh as it were—
was in church. So yes, I come out of a "church form," a term I owe
to Stephen Henderson's introduction to *Understanding the New Black
Poetry*. A church form, but I don't come from the A.M.E. Church
or the Baptists. Elsewhere in the "Negro Artist" essay Hughes dis-
misses black Episcopalians but that's what we were—my parents
still are—and I recall those Sundays listening to our priest, a black
man named M. Bartlett Cochran who came from southern Ohio;
he'd read from the very High-Church *Book of Common Prayer* and,
though he did not change a word of the text, his voice did things not
to the language but *with* it—they met, mingled, engaged each other,
and together created an amazing commotion, a huge early part of
my literary experience. This is Miscegenation Studies. I hear his
voice now as I type this, the timbre of it. I learned the conventional
wisdom a long time ago—to "watch verbs"; but Father Cochran's
emphasis was on the work done by the prepositions, the conjunc-
tions, the adjectives, and from him I learned about the r's at the ends
of words that could stay—meaning *remain*—a vibration at the back
of the mouth. Arr? No, aww(r). "Until the shadows lengthen and
the evening comes and the busy world is hushed and the fever of
life is over and our work is done."

I'm in Michael S. Harper's and Anthony Walton's recently pub-
lished *Vintage Anthology of African-American Verse*, which pleases
me in spite of my powerful ambivalence about anthologies. I'm in
the back of the book next to another of my fellow Ohioans, Rita
Dove. Nathaniel Mackey's in it too—he and I, though, are the only
two from this gang. There are no photographs in this volume, only
descriptions, and I'll confess to being distressed some at the head-
note that begins my section—I'm attributed to (1) the rust belt, (2)
Charles Olson, (3) Ezra Pound, and (4) James Wright.

Now the trouble is that I do claim all those white guys and
that region but my attribution to only white (and regional) sources
denies both for me and for other black "innovative" writers (since
this is a Vintage book and widely distributed and since we're not,
as I mention above, well-represented in it) the sort of past I've been
trying to sketch out here this morning. Being mindful about the
past demands, for me, that I neither deny nor glorify miscegena-
tion—either one—but that I study it and understand that miscege-
nation (the unsaid but common, the everyday truth, the banality)
also studies me. The headnote in the Vintage book makes it seem
that I'm the adopted child of a kind, liberal white family. I've read
Olson but before I read Olson I read Jean Toomer and I've said on
a number of occasions that the work in the anthology (all of which
is from my 1994 book, *Here*) is really a response, an homage, to
Cane, to the literary value Toomer assigned to the black migration
north, to his articulation of that, meaning how he broke all that
down. To be north with the south still in your head after all this
time. One of the poems in *Here* (from the loose, "floating" sequence
that concerns the black Hudson River School painter, Robert S.
Duncanson) is a place where the homage is, I think, particularly
visible. It's included at the end of this piece. (Included here also is
a poem "about" James Wright, also from *Here*. I'm not expecting to
be invited to the annual James Wright festival that's put on by the
Martin's Ferry Public Library.)

The word I get to, vis-à-vis the Vintage book, is from Harryette

Mullen, her word for describing the experimental black writer, "unanticipated." ("She is unanticipated and often unacknowledged due to the imposed obscurity of her aesthetic antecedents.") As I've said elsewhere, in writing about black Canadians, there are "a lot of ways to take the fall and find yourself outside history."

3.
(Shortlidge Rd., Penn State campus, University Park, PA, late April 2000)

Music comes in at the close, like always. Stuck in traffic among twenty-year-olds in BMWs and SUVs, one of the little traffic jams that happens at Penn State when classes change. On the radio, all-oldies-all-the-time, was the Mamas and the Papas' delicate and squeaky "Dedicated to the One I Love." It's this version, their cover, this is the way I first heard the song in 1967 or so, only discovering an earlier version, by the Shirelles, later. (The song was written by Ralph Bass—née Basso—and Lowman Pauling; Pauling was the guitarist for The "5" Royales, who first recorded the song.)

James Wright's "Minneapolis Poem," which I reference in my poem to him below, includes the passage,

> *Tall Negro girls from Chicago*
> *Listen to light songs.*
> *They know when the supposed patron*
> *Is a plainclothesman.*

Wright's poetry "lacks discipline," according to some critics; this is noted, among other more salutary descriptions of the work, on the poetryfoundation.org website where "The Minneapolis Poem" is categorized as "Crime & Punishment, Cities & Urban Life, Social Commentaries, Money & Economics, Race & Ethnicity"; on the website each category is linked to other poems having to do with the same issues. "The Minneapolis Poem" appears in *Shall We Gather at the River* (which title is a reference to "a favorite song of camp meetings, water baptismal services and funerals"), published in 1968. The '60s was the era of the Shirelles—the four girls from New Jersey (Shirley Owens, Doris Coley, Addie "Micki" Harris, and Beverly Lee), together, wrote "I Met Him on a Sunday" for a talent show at their high school. They released "Dedicated to the One I Love" twice, first in 1959 and again in 1961. The Shirelles, often heralded as the first "girl group," debuted at the Apollo and—according to their website—headlined "the first integrated show in Alabama." I heard and remember having heard "Mama Said" in 1961, on the radio, when I was ten. The article in the *San Francisco Chronicle* says that the group, or a fragment of it, "survived the lean years working Caribbean resorts and European military bases." In 1961 they had half-sung and half-declared:

> *Mama said there'll be days like this,*
> *There'll be days like this, Mama said.*
> *Mama said there'll be days like this,*
> *There'll be days like this,*
> *My Mama said.*

"Mama Said" was written by Luther Dixon, who had learned to sing in church; according to the Chancellor of Soul's *Soul Facts Show* it was "inspired by his great grandmother." Dixon's obituary in the *Independent* noted that "[t]here had been few successful black girl groups before the Shirelles, but such acts now became a permanent feature of the pop charts." Numerous girl groups rose through the decade—the Marvelettes, the Shangri-Las (a trio of "bad white girls"), the Supremes of course, and Martha Reeves and the Vandellas. "Has high blood pressure got a hold on me," Martha Reeves sang, "or is this the way love's supposed to be?" Carole King and Gerry Goffin also wrote for the Shirelles—notably "Will You Still Love Me Tomorrow?"—as did Burt Bacharach.

If there's a reading strategy there's a listening strategy; there are ways of paying attention. "What are you *quoting*?" I asked the Mamas and the Papas. What's being traced here, and in what hand?

———————————

Two Poems from *Here*:

DUNCANSON'S "VIEW OF CINCINNATI, OHIO FROM COVINGTON, KENTUCKY," 1848

The wide eye corporeal &
at the time sane, both—

but on the remotest edge

of description, at an unexaggerated pinnacle

of the color line,

at no rest, no rest, no Campground

to come between the long stare across

& the big pale sky

no place for the eye to rest on, soul's

opaque surface

or the river sloped down to
by Covington houses

or Ohio's dim self of hills & smoke, another economy

TO JAMES WRIGHT

Way over on my far side of the river we could hear

in Martha Reeves' voice the thing beyond what the music took,
what
little it could take,

the hard quaver of inflection

(beyond "verbal play"

raised into pure incredulity (her
rhetorical *is this?   is this?   is this?*

her voice in the voices of regular girls I knew
when they'd talk
loud among themselves on the way home
walking home from 8th grade (or their voices in hers,

she was almost as young then herself as we were:

Negro girls from where? listen to what? knowing
    what?

(1964, 1965 *post-innocence*
(if barely

(sweat beading over broken hearts being the way

NORTH / STATEMENT FOR *XCP*

North—

Facts beyond the set of destinations. In terms of direction, the opposite of south; conventionally mapped as superior.

In terms of black subjectivity, north is most contradictory among directions: race (beyond destination) is multiple, ambiguous, and anecdotal, not storied. Yet north is (and has been) the racial figure for an open gate or series. If south is (or can be) "where the Southern cross the Yellow Dog" (W. C. Handy), north needs music.

The fact of great migration, the trope north.

Belligerently, "our northern neighbor." Ishmael Reed: "He preferred Canada to slavery, whether Canada was exile, death, art, liberation, or a woman." Margaret Atwood's *Surfacing*: "nothing in the North but the past and not much of that either . . ." Steve McCaffery: "North of intention."

In terms of vernacular and measure north is opaque, unfamiliar (not "back north," e.g.), final and open at once.

THREE NOTES ON MONSTERS

1. Letter to Arielle Greenberg Concerning 1977

Dear Arielle—1977? I lived in Syracuse and saw Rocky fight Carl Weathers at the multiplex at Shoppingtown, glorious lost cause, and Travolta outdance the competition's dark campaign at one at the Fayetteville Mall. Saw economic recovery in *The Marriage of Maria Braun*, this at the Manlius Cinema, and turned saying—having to—"kindly shut the fuck up" to the man complaining about Hanna Schygulla's black lover. (The E! website drops the lie on memory— this was 1979 and only feels like it was 1977, that memory thing that carries right on over from one to the next, that pours across the border. No name for the black actor anywhere on the web.) But saw Duane Jones dominate *Night of the Living Dead* downtown at the Civic Center's Halloween Movie Marathon, truly 1977, the film having come out nine years previous, having earned a rep but for other stuff than Duane Jones. Faux nostalgia then and nowadays for the whitest zombie cannibals in us all; faux nostalgic paeans to white hopes on the dance stage and in the cinematic ring. But at the Civic Center the ambiguity of blackness went riding to the center of the screen for once, a repeat and revise on Lowell's "to choose life and die": when he shoots the white zombies to death, he does not go all stiff. Made near Greensburg, PA in 1968, Arielle, not 1977 but seen by yours truly for the first time in 1977 at the Civic Center in Syracuse. Your town and my town.—C.

2. Rejected by the *New Yorker*

Saturday morning, the second day of the impeachment debate in the House of Representatives, but I was ignoring that and sitting

downstairs in our house working at the computer and watching the
flock of juncos squabbling around the feeder. My wife was upstairs,
following the debate on the radio; a little after ten o'clock she came
down to tell me that Bob Livingston of Louisiana, the speaker-des-
ignate, had just declined the speaker's post and that in fact he was
going to ask the governor of Louisiana to replace him in Congress
itself by calling a special election, this in response to the facts of
his marital infidelity becoming public. He'd said he was resigning,
Katharine told me, as an example to the country, as a challenge to
the President to do the right thing. We shook our heads over this,
a little stunned at what we both understood to be the depths of the
Republicans' hatred of Clinton, and then she went back upstairs
and I returned to the computer.

   I had been working on a piece of writing that contained sev-
eral movie references and, in light of the news from Washington, I
skimmed it idly and wondered *What kind of film is this impeachment
going to be in a couple of years?* Spike Lee's already been fairly brilliant
about what doing the right thing means. I don't think there's going
to be another *All the President's Men*. I recalled watching the ulti-
mate film account of a great culture brought to its knees by sexual
turpitude, *Birth of a Nation*. But I found myself thinking finally
about last year's *Alien* series movie, *The Resurrection*: I insisted on
reading the film as a smart "passing" narrative (much to the amuse-
ment of my students in the African-American Literature course I
was teaching when the film came out, a course in which we were
in fact reading Nella Larsen's novel, *Passing*). Neither of the princi-
pals, Sigourney Weaver and Winona Ryder, were the straight, white,
heterosexual, human women they appeared to be: there was a secret
hidden in both their blood. But it was the blood of the monsters in
the film that I was thinking about as I turned away from the mon-
itor and gazed outside at the birds. From upstairs Katharine's radio
was a faint murmur.

   In the movie, scientists on a spaceship are keeping monsters—
the aliens of the title—locked up in a metal cell but the monsters

realize at some point that their blood is acid and can eat through metal. In hulking gestures on the screen they form a monster covenant and two of them rip a third to shreds: the copious blood that results from that eats away at their confines and the two remaining are free to pursue their agenda among the inhabitants of the ship.

3. Improvisation

To improvise may be to spontaneously compose and perform but it's possible to break that down. *Compose* (or its noun, composition) implies disparate parts; *perform* is to speak the parts aloud, to make the loud display. (Spontaneity's a kind of magic or at least a flash.) Where's the language of the improvisation itself come from? Down deep inside or from some shallow depth? But before it was down in there it was outside and that's my interest, the parts and how they got in. To me, improvisation is a series of references, one building on the one previous but also the statement of meeting the other and what happens when that happens.

I'm interested in the horror-film genre for lots of reasons not least of which is its emphasis on how bodies appear and mutate, what secrets they hide, this being obviously an old racial interest. I'm interested in how we, black people, appear in horror. Nowadays we get to be Candyman or Blacula (or monster food in *Jurassic Park*) but back in the day we were an oblique reference. I'm thinking today of John Carradine as the title character in *House of Dracula*, an old favorite from 1945. In the "piano scene"—as it's described on YouTube—Dracula comes to see the doctor's lovely assistant (Miliza Morrelle, played by Martha O'Driscoll) while the doctor's out. This is my favorite cinematic depiction of improvisation.

In the scene Ms. O'Driscoll is at the piano, playing the "Moonlight Sonata"; but when the vampire appears in the drawing room and begins a conversation with her the music changes, becomes jazz.

"Baron," she says, startled, "I didn't hear you come in."

And then, as the music changes, "I never heard this music before and yet I'm playing it."

Mr. Carradine responds, "You're creating it—for me."

The music frightens her, she says, and her speech goes on in that vein—"It calls to me, but I'm afraid."

The music becomes more interesting, more intense, but then she reaches into her cleavage and pulls out a crucifix, which makes Mr. Carradine's character turn away, at which point the "Moonlight Sonata" resumes.

She was playing that white music ("a little of the Ludwig Van") but then under the spell of Transylvania Fever she just about left that whiteness behind and was gonna *be* the Vamp of Savannah. Luckily Lord Jesus emerged from her underwear to save her and all of us.

LYCANTHROPY

Lycanthropy is, at once, a fear and a presentiment (the latter term suggested by Captain Marryat); as well, lycanthropy is cognizance, frank in its appearance, of the facts of human shapes (and interest) and the relation of such shapes to broad categories, notably to the varieties of animal life. This—the troubling matter of awareness—can occur as a sharp, or sudden, insight or one that overtakes its subject slowly. Or lycanthropy may occur as an expository act of recollection, an attribution, a paean, or a truce. At its base lycanthropy is an uneasy companionship; that is, lycanthropy mirrors.

Relying heavily on the work of Mary Henrietta Kingsley, Sir James George Frazer (1922) reported that, "[the] negroes of Calabar, at the mouth of the Niger, believe that every person has four souls, one of which always lives outside of his or her body in the form of a wild beast in the forest. This external soul, or bush soul, . . . may be almost any animal, for example, a leopard, a fish, or a tortoise; but it is never a domestic animal and never a plant." L. W. G. Malcolm (1922) wrote of the problems "concerning the trapping of a man's ukpōñ, or bush-soul as it is more commonly called" and noted that "[the] explanation of the Efik belief in the bush-soul is somewhat difficult to understand." In *the Dictionary of the Efik Language*, however, compiled by Hugh Goldie (1874), ukpōñ has three definitions—the first is "[the] shadow of a person or thing which moves" and the second is "[the] soul of man." The third definition is of particular interest here: "An animal, with the existence of which the life of the individual is bound up. It may be a leopard, a fish, a crocodile, any animal whatever . . ."; the third definition continues with the observation that "[many] individuals, it is believed, have the power of metamorphosing themselves into their ukpōñ."

In Greek mythology Lycaon or Lykaon, a king, had contrived to test the divinity of Zeus by serving the god a slaughtered child and Zeus, in agitation, transformed the king into a wolf. This story is often cited as the source of the term at hand, lycanthropy, but lycanthropy is, in fact, from the Greek words for wolf ("lukos") and human being or man ("anthrōpos"). The first definition in the *Oxford English Dictionary* begins, "A kind of insanity"; the second—"The kind of witchcraft which was supposed to consist in the assumption by human beings of the form and nature of wolves." The *OED* citations include Reginald Scot (1684)—"Lycanthropia is a disease and not a transformation"—and *The Anatomy of Melancholy* (1621), in which Richard Burton describes the affliction as, "Woolfe madness, when men run howling about graues and fields in the night, and will not be perswaded but that they are Wolues, or some such beasts." Yet Burton excepts lycanthropy from the ranges of melancholy—"I should rather referre it to madnesse, as most doe"—and adds that "[s]ome make a doubt of it whether there be any such disease." Montague Summers refers to Reginald Scot's book, *Discoverie of Witchcraft*, as "notorious," yet provides no definition of the pejorative. The *OED*'s second definition of lycanthrope states, "By mod. writers used as a synonym of werewolf."

Summers, in *The Werewolf* (1933), states: "It should be remarked that in a secondary or derivative sense the word werewolf has been erroneously employed to denote a person suffering from lycanthropy, that mania or disease when the patient imagines himself to be a wolf, and under that savage delusion betrays all the bestial propensities of the wolf, howling in a horrid long drawn out note. This madness will hardly at all concern us here." The subject of Summers's study is the establishment of observable or observed fact. He writes, "From whatever cause this shape-shifting may arise, it is very certain by the common consent of all antiquity and all history, by the testimony of learned men, by experience and first-hand witness, that werewolfism which involves some change of form from man to animal is a very real and very terrible thing." Summers concludes with a question: "What do we see when we espy a werewolf? Sometimes we behold a real body, not created but newly formed from existing elements by Satan; sometimes it is a fantastical shape." And Peter Fleming (1931) wryly notes, "All through the Middle Ages, down to the seventeenth century, there were innumerable cases (especially in France) of men and women being legally tried for offenses which they had committed as animals. Like the witches, they were rarely acquitted, but, unlike the witches, they seem seldom to have been unjustly condemned."

Fleming and others note that the index fingers of lycanthropes— when they are in human form or guise—are as long as or longer than their middle fingers. James Fiske, writing in the *Atlantic* (1871), remarks that it was popularly believed that some lycanthropes enabled their transformation into wolves by putting on a girdle made of human skin. Fiske recounts an incident in which a child found his father's girdle and, curious, donned it, at which point he was transformed. The father, returning home, took stock of the situation and "restored the child to his natural shape." Fiske notes, "The boy said that no sooner had he buckled it on than he was tormented with a raging hunger." In *that they were at the beach* (1985) Leslie Scalapino describes a surreptitiously observed scene: "She heard the sounds of a couple having intercourse and then getting up they went into the shower so that she caught a sight of them naked before hearing the water running. The parts of their bodies which had been covered by clothes were those of leopards. During puberty her own organs and skin were not like this though when she had first had intercourse with a man he removed his clothes and his organ and flesh were also a leopard's."

The "amorous entertangling" of pleasure and disgust is part of the notable sexuality associated with lycanthropy. That range encompasses much—lycanthropy has been cast, by turns, as sacrificial and fearful (on one hand) and powerful (on another). The ambiguity of sexual roles itself is central to lycanthropy, as is the unstable bridge between the vagaries of human nature and "the amoral lives of animals," as Joseph Martin (1980) put it. Lycanthropy, by its nature, addresses the wished-for but unavailable closure that reparation is imagined to provide—lycanthropy is unforgivable and unforgiving.

Sometimes the victim of a lycanthrope is consumed by his or her attacker. If lycanthropy is a dream, the familiar trick of asking a single question of the dream seldom produces results—the presentiment has been variously described but tomorrow's answer never comes.

Lycanthropy has, since the early twentieth century, garnered interest from the movie industry. Warner Oland was the first white man to play a self-aware lycanthrope—"the mysterious Doctor Yogami," a composite of Asian identities—in a sound film, *Werewolf of London* (1935). Oland, who was cast "opposite" the title character, portrayed by Henry Hull, had played Papa Rabinowitz in *The Jazz Singer* (1927) and went on to play the "Chinese" detective Charlie Chan in a number of films. He—Warner Oland—was Swedish but was often called upon to portray "ethnic" characters. As Doctor Yogami in wolf-guise Oland bites Henry Hull's forearm early in the film and, that way, passes his infection on to Hull. Both *Cat People* films (Jacques Tourneur, 1942; Paul Schrader, 1982) involve European women who transform into leopards. In the later version the black actor Ruby Dee—who plays the knowing servant of a lycanthropic white man—advises the white star, Nastassja Kinski, that she can cope with her curse if she is willing to live "in chains."

There is, in fact, little good that can be said about psychological healing, though it is often stated popularly that time heals wounds and that there exists a pure good feeling when one forgets some troublesome memory. The comparative "lesson" is to flesh—that skin closes over a wound and makes one whole again, as though the incident that opened the skin had never, in fact, occurred. In fact, the lycanthrope's script provides its speaker with no information, only that she or he is "a nocturnal wanderer" who has had a presentiment that the evening will come to grief (or encounter grief). Lycanthropy, in fact or fable, is a bad debt. Lycanthropy has no value, practically speaking, as instruction or example and is, in fact, an endless rage.

Robert Eisler, in the notes on *Man into Wolf* (1951), makes casual reference to "the sadist 'Lady in the Fur,' now with the added charm for the masochist of blood-red varnished, needle-pointed nails, looking as if she had just indulged in an omophagic orgy of tearing live animals to pieces . . ."; he continues—"As to the nails varnished so as to look bloodstained, they are said to have been invented by Creole women anxious to hide under the opaque colour the tell-tale dark crescent betraying an admixture of Negro blood."

No one has written more wisely about lycanthropy than Angela Carter.

Entre chien et loup is the phrase for early evening or dusk, a time when it is not possible to definitively identify the animal in the near distance. Early evening—the stage between afternoon and dark—is an overlapping passage; it is different than the golden hour or *l'heure bleue*. Dusk, often storied as an opening to songs of anticipation, is the latter part of twilight. The gloaming is "dusky light"; Andrew Irving (2013) writes, "The gloaming does not wholly belong to the visibility of day or the invisibility of night but mediates the two by retaining traces of daylight and a presentiment of the darkness to come or vice versa." *Crepuscular* pertains to twilight, broadly defined; predatory animals are often crepuscular.

INTRODUCTION TO *AMERICAN BOOK REVIEW*'S FOCUS ON INNOVATIVE POETRY (SUMMER 2005)

One needs in late 2005 to begin any announcement about innovation or "difficult poetry" with an acknowledgment of the life and work and example of Robert Creeley, who died at the end of March, who was—in Olson's phrase—"the figure of outward." He wrote, in 1964, "I am wary of any didactic program for the arts and yet I cannot ignore the fact that poetry, in my own terms of experience, obtains to an unequivocal order. What I deny, then, is any assumption that that order can be either acknowledged or gained by intellectual assertion, or will, or some like intention to shape language to a purpose which the literal act of writing does not itself discover."

Forty-one springs later this special section has come together quickly, and the focus—though still on the fact of discovery—is not encyclopedic or even representative of the varieties of work out there. My impulse is to apologize for the books not reviewed here—I think in particular of the new volumes by Will Alexander, Leslie Scalapino, Pierre Joris, Mark Wallace, Wanda Coleman, Peter Gizzi, the incomparable Bernadette Mayer. And David McAleavey's *Huge Haiku*, Ron Silliman's *Under Albany*, and certainly *Integral Music: Languages of African-American Innovation*, by my homeboy Aldon Lynn Nielsen. But such apologies are useless and beside the point; we'll try to get to the books mentioned above in the next issues. This may be the special focus on innovative writing but *ABR*'s traffic with the innovative is only useful because it's ongoing.

Now what might innovation mean? I recently wrote that elements of such poetry—language as topic, its opacity and juxtapositions, its failures and samplings, etc.—were themselves useful for troubling ideas of the "intimacy" of literature. That's not the

be-all/end-all but let it stand, like an open door, for now. One does
what one must do. Out in the street the poetry wars continue.
Garrison Keillor's whites-only anthology, *Good Poems*, is still selling
briskly this year and stodgy old *Poetry* magazine has been gifted with
enough pharmaceutical millions to maintain its high profile. You'll
not see work by Juliana Spahr, Renee Gladman, Gillian Conley,
Taylor Brady, Barry McKinnon, or Ken Belford there. Of course,
Amiri Baraka's "Someone Blew Up America" certainly has gotten
some press; it's the poem most discussed in the recent newspapers,
the most publicized poem of the twenty-first century. Yet none of
the papers reprinted it or quoted it to any extent or suggested that
the poem had an argument (beyond anti-Semitism) or any music
or that its argument (that state terrorism exists and that the West is
and has been a perpetrator of it) might be worth bothering about.

It's June 2005 and I'm back in the States, back from AWP in
Vancouver where I was in on two events—a panel titled "Writing the
North," about a poetics of the Canadian bush, and a group reading
by contributors (I was one) to the anthology *Bluesprint: Black British
Columbian Literature and Orature*. These are two items—blackness
and Canada—that make uneasy bedfellows with everyday notions
of the innovative and I wanted to make sure that that connection
was spoken to in these reviews. On the "Writing the North" panel,
Ken Belford—whose new book is under review here—said, "Finally
we have a land poetics that isn't naive, in the way so much of the
rural poetry has been. In lan(d)guage poetry we have a poetics that
doesn't impose the heavy hand of place-ism on the writer." Renee
Gladman was not in attendance in Vancouver. But in an essay in
the 2001 issue of *Tripwire* devoted to African-American writing,
she pointed out that "[a]ny writer, not just the marginalized one,
communicates his or her cultural or racial perspective in his or her
work. Even in the avant-garde."

AWP itself was a paean to comfort—the writers who were there
were handsome and well-dressed and well-behaved and spent appro-
priately in the upscale eateries. The creative writing industry has

certainly come along. We did not riot in Robson Street to demand that Canada accept military refugees from the American war in Iraq; nor we did not pass out incomprehensible leaflets.

My thanks to the reviewers who responded to my requests to get work together quickly. And my thanks to Charles Harris and to Lisa Savage for this opportunity.

OUR VARIOUSNESS

This writing is designed as a prologue, a statement of concern(s), a catalogue, diatribe, caution, essay, and manifesto. The field of concern is the ongoing presence, in Nova Scotia, of a visible (meaning sizable, meaning vocal or capable of making itself heard, if locally) black population, one with origins in the eighteenth- and nineteenth-century troubles between Britain and the United States. Though this population's American descent is not unique in Canada (northbound black groups and individuals have been crossing the U.S./Canadian border through the centuries) it's of special interest because the population's numbers began with the American Revolution.

This is a prologue then to an as-yet unspecified and undefined response to both the *presence Africadian* (George Elliott Clarke's term)[1] and to the absence of talk about this population in the discourses of the United States. That is, the fact of black Nova Scotians with historically interesting roots in the United States is not, generally speaking, discussed in African-American letters or popular discourse and it is not (generally speaking) represented or referenced in the media controlled by white American interests. My response—as an African-American writer concerned with borders, the myth of authenticity, relations with the "bigger man," and with the problems of narrative and image—will be in the form of prose, some inventive relation of fiction to non-fiction; it will be a dance that will, to the best of my abilities, engage the conditions and the silence. This writing, below, is an attempt—the essay—at laying out the range of those conditions (including the silences).

1.

Start with the map. This one, provided by the Nova Scotia Museum's

website, is a general-reference map: if the world of cartography could
be divided into two genres of mapping they might be general-refer-
ence and thematic, the latter referring to maps "used to emphasize
the spatial distribution of one or more geographic attributes," such
as "different magnitudes of a variable" (Slocum 3). But this—in
spite of being partially keyed to a web exhibit—is general-reference,
a statement of locations:

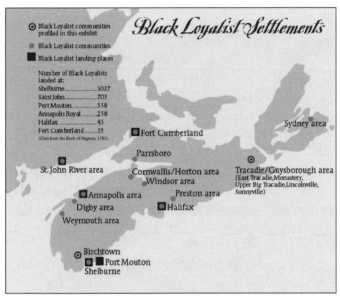

(Nova Scotia Museum)

The variables' magnitude doesn't change. The theme's the theme
but the statement the map makes bears some explanation. "Black
Loyalists" is the name that has come to represent the group of black
Americans who came to Nova Scotia in the 1780s, this part of the
fallout from the American Revolution.

"Judging slavery to be a major weakness of the rebellious southern
colonies," Robin Winks wrote, "the British offered emancipation
to all slaves who, during the revolution, volunteered to serve with
their forces" (Winks 29). The first offer came in November 1775

from John Murray, Lord Dunmore, Governor of Virginia. Dunmore declared "all indented servants, negroes, or others (appertaining to Rebels) free, that are able and willing to bear arms, they joining his Majesty's troops, as soon as may be, for the more speedily reducing this Colony to a proper sense of their duty, to his Majesty's crown and dignity" (Walker 1). The qualification, the parenthetical "appertaining to Rebels," is important. Planters and others loyal to the Crown (including Dunmore) *kept* their blacks. However, Walker continues, "[w]hen he met the rebels at Great Bridge on 9 December, one half of Dunmore's troops consisted of runaway slaves" (Walker 1). The British were not being altruistic. Simon Schama cautions that "[t]he promise was made for military rather humanitarian purposes" (Schama 15) and notes that "[t]he contortions of logic were so perverse, yet so habitual, that George Washington"—who had been friends with Dunmore in Virginia— "could describe [him] as 'that arch traitor to the rights of humanity' for promising to free slaves and indentured servants, whilst those who kept them in bondage were heroes to liberty" (Schama 15). Later, in 1779, the British Commander in Chief, Sir Henry Clinton, repeating and revising Dunmore, promised this:

> [T]o every NEGRO who shall desert the Rebel Standard, full security to follow within these Lines, and Occupation which he shall think proper. (Walker 2)

What this—Clinton's promise, the Phillipsburg Proclamation—did was to open up the British lines as a place of refuge to all slaves, not just those who could bear arms. Again, there was no altruism here but a calculation to wreck the economy of the Colonies, which was slave-labor dependent. Be that as it may be, the proclamation would prove important later.

What eighteenth-century American slaves did was to weigh options. "The number of Negroes who fled to the British ran into the tens of thousands," said Benjamin Quarles (Quarles 119). And

Herbert Aptheker: "[I]t appears to be conservative to say that from 1775 to 1783 some one hundred thousand slaves (i.e., about one out of every five) *succeeded* in escaping from slavery, though very often meeting death or serfdom instead of liberty" (Italics Aptheker's; Aptheker 20). Sylvia Frey: "It is difficult to say with precision how many slaves actually left their owners. Estimates range from eighty thousand to one hundred thousand. The exact number is, at any rate, less important than the general changes their departures produced" (Frey 211). Black people who had run off worked for the British as soldiers, laborers, spies, pilots. Colonies passed laws against this and South Carolina and Virginia executed slaves for it; others were sold offshore. Some—actually rather many—died of disease: smallpox was a big problem. And others melted in after the war with the free black populations. But after all was said and done, something in excess of three thousand people ended up in New York listed in the British Commander-in-Chief's "Book of Negroes," and were evacuated north to Nova Scotia, consequence of their actions, this in 1783.

Of course the exodus was, racially speaking, complex. Simon Schama: "Around fifteen percent of the incoming loyalists to Nova Scotia were black—perhaps five thousand in all—although only half to two-thirds came as free Britons, emancipated through their war service (some others among the euphemistically designated 'servants' were given their freedom on arrival)" (Schama 231–2). The white Loyalists, in other words, brought their slaves with them.

In the War of 1812 the Americans faced Britain again. Washington, D.C. was burned and British ships blockaded the mid-Atlantic coast, this to cripple American commerce with Europe. And once again, the British targeted the slaves with promises of freedom:

> Hundreds of Blacks in the Chesapeake Bay states as well as in other areas of the British blockade seized their opportunity and made their way to the British vessels and the promised

freedom. The British, knowing that the removal of slaves would reduce the affected area's contribution to the war effort, liberated several thousand . . . The number of slaves freed included those who had escaped on their own initiative, those who were encouraged by their fellows (sent back for that purpose) to escape, and those who had freedom forced on them as a result of the continuous raids of the British marines. (Grant 22)

The ex-slaves were recruited as soldiers and sent back (they went eagerly) to advance the British cause against the Americans. On 4 August 1814 a petition from white Virginians to the American Adjutant General complained thus:

Our negroes are flocking to the enemy from all quarters, which they convert into troops, vindictive and rapacious—with a minute knowledge of every by-path. They leave us as spies upon our strength and return to us as guides and soldiers and incendiaries. (Grant 22)

Some of the slaves freed by the British went to Trinidad and other locations in the West Indies, but once again the bulk—about 2,000 people—ended up in Nova Scotia. It's from this group that most (though by no means all) present-day black Nova Scotians—the Africadians—are descended (Winks 127).

The references start early. Barry Cahill notes that "[t]he earliest usage of the term 'Negro Loyalists' that I am aware of occurs in the writings of Thomas Chandler Haliburton," and he references the author's 1829 book, *An Historical and Statistical Account of Nova Scotia* (Cahill 78). Or Kipling's 1896 *Captains Courageous*: "'His natural tongue's kinder curious. Comes from the in'ards of Cape Breton, he does, where the farmers speak home-made Scotch. Cape Breton's full o' niggers whose folk run in there durin' aour war, an' they talk like the farmers—all huffy-chuffy'" (Kipling 403). In *The Blacks in Canada* Robin Winks, accounting for the scattering of African-descended people through Ontario and Quebec and the Maritimes after the Revolutionary War, notes that ". . . by far the greatest number went to Nova Scotia, and there the majority were free men. Thinking themselves Loyalists, many felt entitled to the same benefits that a grateful King gave his white subjects" (Winks 35). Again, the qualification—Winks's insistence that Loyalist status is an instance of *self-description*—is important.

The black Loyalists—the people who arrived in 1783—found Nova Scotia to be a place of some difficulty. They encountered an unfair distribution of provisions and they discovered that the land—promised by the British—went first and in bigger parcels to the white Loyalists. They maintained but did so at considerable disadvantage to their white compatriots. Schama: "That through being made landless and hungry free blacks had been forced into indentures so punitive that they might as well be in chains" (Schama 219). When John Clarkson, representing the Sierra Leone Company, traveled Nova Scotia in 1791 recruiting dissatisfied Africadians for the project of settling that colony, he found much interest, and in 1792 about 1200 people left Halifax harbor for the coast of Africa and did not come back to Nova Scotia.

This exodus—the fact of the return (or the "return") to Africa in 1792—has been the focus or the agreed-upon end point of what little writing there is about the black Loyalists. This is full circle, this is closure. Ellen Gibson Wilson begins *The Loyal Blacks* with "a fleet of fifteen sailing ships [dropping] anchor in the mouth of the Sierra Leone River and [disembarking] 1100 men, women, and children on a bush-covered shore which had just been named Freetown"—the book then traces the chain of events leading up (through the war and Nova Scotia) to this initial image (Gibson ix). Wallace Brown observes that "[t]he history of American blacks after the Revolution is not a happy one" (Brown 126). And he goes on, documenting that: "In British North America, slavery died out in the early nineteenth century, but the hapless free blacks remained at the fringes of white society. The only bright spot was Sierra Leone where . .

. American blacks and their descendants maintained a privileged, fairly prosperous position until the present" (Brown 126). Nova Scotia—in Walker's landmark *The Black Loyalists* and in Schama's *Rough Crossings*—has been cast as a jumping-off place, a place to tarry and suffer and kill time until the transport back to the place of origin arrived. A waiting room as it were. But not everyone went to Sierra Leone.

In 1999 the *New York Times*, the newspaper of record in the U.S., "discovered" the black Loyalists. "For Nova Scotia Blacks, Veil is Ripped from the Past," crowed the headline on the International News page (Brooke 4). The writer interviewed Everett and Elizabeth Cromwell, black residents of Shelburne-Birchtown, where the Loyalists landed in 1783; an unnamed informant, apparently from the Nova Scotia Museum, had recently shown Mr. Cromwell, a native Nova Scotian who professed to know little about the province's black past, a copy of the "Book of Negroes" and had acquainted him with enough history for Mr. Cromwell to make a statement to the *New York Times*:

> "When they fought the Americans for the British, as far as they were concerned, they were fighting for their freedom," said Mr. Cromwell, 77, who fought alongside American units in Europe in World War II. (Brooke 4)

The quotation is interesting in that it boasts two qualifications—Mr. Cromwell's and the writer's—and these play off one another. Mr. Cromwell is shown to have been on the "right" side, important even in those pre-9/11 days, in another historical conflict. The obvious question—about whether he encountered the racism and discrimination that was part and parcel of the U.S. Army of the 1940s—does not arise. Mr. Cromwell's own quite ambiguous "as far as they were concerned," read in context of his battlefield experience alongside Americans in "the Good War," loses any sting it might have had and *appears* dismissive.

The article's interesting for other reasons as well. It suggests that there is some difference between Tories and Loyalists ("Determined to hold on to Canada, the British populated Nova Scotia with people hostile to the American Revolution—decommissioned British soldiers, white Tories, and black Loyalists."), this presumably for American readers used to hearing the former term and not the latter (Brooke 40). And it implies that Canada—a well-known-for-centuries haven for blacks—has not done well or honestly by its African-descended population by keeping them in ignorance about their past. "After two centuries of neglect bordering on denial, Nova Scotia now is unearthing its black history," states the fourth paragraph (Brooke 4). But both white and black Americans are, generally speaking, *quite* ignorant of there having been black Loyalists or Tories. The headline could have interposed the word "Americans" for "Blacks" and the statement about the veil being ripped aside would have been *at least* as true.

Americans are let off the hook, though, while the *Times* gets Hegelian on the Africadians. "For Hegel . . . , cast into silence by their own loss or absence of voice, Africans could have no history, no meaningful text of blackness itself, since they had no true self-consciousness, no power to present or represent this black and terrible self" (Gates 104). There are, of course, many ambiguous ways to take the fall and find oneself outside history.

But finally there's the choice of *veil*, a highly racialized term. For Du Bois it was a metaphor for both race and for the racial divide itself. "After the Egyptian and Indian, the Greek and Roman, the Teuton and Mongolian," he wrote, "the Negro is a sort of seventh son, born with a veil, and gifted with second-sight in this American world . . ." (Du Bois 8). Du Bois's metaphor is ambiguous enough and well-known enough to be the topic of many dreary term papers but it's the famous Tuskegee Institute statue of Booker T. Washington (Du Bois's nemesis) that the newspaper seems to traffic more directly with. Ralph Ellison evokes it in *Invisible Man*:

Then in my mind's eye I see the bronze statue of the college
Founder, the cold Father symbol, his hands outstretched in the
breathtaking gesture of lifting a veil that flutters in hard, metal-
lic folds above the face of a kneeling slave; and I am standing
puzzled, unable to decide whether the veil is being really lifted,
or lowered more firmly in place; whether I am witnessing a
revelation or a more efficient blinding. (Ellison 36)

2.

In February 2006 I arrived in Halifax, my arrival made possible
by a Faculty Research Grant from the Canadian Embassy, and I
was welcomed warmly by the Gorsebrook Research Institute at St.
Mary's University. My interest was primarily the history and survival
in Nova Scotia of the black Loyalist group, the people whose exodus
from the U.S. in the eighteenth century has been effectively made
a non-event in American—and African-American—historical con-
sciousness; this is the "ignorance" I allude to just above. (I base these
statements on my own casual survey, made at academic gatherings
and conferences—and in classrooms—over the past three or four
years in a variety of U.S. locations; I've asked, at seminar tables and
from podiums, for a show of hands to indicate how many people
know of the British offer and the black response to it. Invariably
the raised hands are few.) My interest in this group—partially at
the expense of the Black Refugees from the War of 1812—has
been twofold. In part, I'm drawn to them simply because they—or,
more correctly, their descendants and partisans—have been vocal
and have done much, thus far, to make themselves visible and, in
that way, have troubled the power statement of historical truth.
("History is the memory of states," said Henry Kissinger [Zinn 9].)
A second reason for this interest is that in this group's dissent from
the Revolution, they bring the most to bear—if symbolically—on
the founding myths of the United States, the ones that we still

symbolize, enshrine, problematize, and labor under more than two hundred years later. "Among the Americans who were prominent in the articulation of the Declaration of Independence as a charter of human liberty, James Madison, Benjamin Harrison, Arthur Middleton and George Washington himself all lost slaves who fled to the banner of British security, many of them seeing active service against the Republican cause" (Walker 4).

I would argue that here in the States Crispus Attucks is *the* black name, the black *personality*, in our common memory of eighteenth-century revolutionary America. The Johnson Publishing Company's history of black soldiers starts with him (Greene 3–5). And on a website, mootstormfront.org, apparently put up to counter the white-supremacist presence on the net, the webmasters quote James Neyland's biography, *Crispus Attucks, Patriot*, a book written for children: "He is one of the most important figures in African-American history, not for what he did for his own race but for what he did for all oppressed people everywhere. He is a reminder that the African-American heritage is not only African but American and it is a heritage that begins with the beginning of America." The webmaster goes on, beyond the text: "Although obscure in life, Attucks played an important role in U.S. history through his death."[2]

Now, we're moviegoers at my house, and some time ago we isolated a sixth American black screen archetype, this beyond Donald Bogle's list (Bogle 3)—the sacrificial black. The sacrificial black's death advances the plot. Examples pulled from recent films might include Samuel L. Jackson in *Jurassic Park*, or Scatman Crothers in *The Shining*, or Joe Morton in the second *Terminator*, or Yaphet Kotto in *Alien*, or Yaphet Kotto in *Blue Collar*. You know it's an archetype when the movies themselves start to refer to it—take note of LL Cool J's speech in which he resolves that he's *not* going to end up as shark food, this in the otherwise unforgivable *Deep Blue Sea*. That my list includes several horror films is less than accidental: I take horror to be a genre in which the subconscious making its way to the surface is privileged. A long time ago—in the intro to *Native*

Son—Richard Wright said if Poe was living now, "horror would invent him" (Wright xxxiv). And I take the sacrificial black archetype rather seriously—it didn't come out of nowhere; it's less a revelation or reflection of something physically threatening or violent in the American psyche than it is of something psychologically flat in the American hierarchy of acceptable loss, of the "necessary" loss that the phrase "collateral damage" covers. If American history is a movie, Crispus Attucks is the sacrificial black. Your job is to die, my brother. This is also what we mean by *closure*.

But Paul Gilroy brought up another description. He said, ". . . we can locate Crispus Attucks at the head of his 'motley rabble of saucy boys, negroes, mulattoes, Irish teagues and outlandish jack tars'" (Gilroy 13). The source of his quotation is John Adams—not yet the second president—who defended in court the British soldiers who killed Attucks and several others; they copped a plea and got off with having their thumbs branded. Adams's speech indicates the unsavory nature of Attucks's associates but Gilroy's point is that the list reveals itself to be made up of marginal travelers on the ocean, a cast with international implications, a shout about multiplicity and the fluidity of association itself. This is a part of *The Black Atlantic's* paean to ships—a Gilroy motif—and Atlantic (or trans-Atlantic) traffic and it's compelling. It takes us *beyond* closure, it denies the fatal and at the same time reveals the "catalyst" mask that ugly (meaning banal and expedient) fatality so often wears. And Gilroy's verb, "locate," offers much in terms of metaphor.

It takes us to Atlantic Canada. If ethnicity and national identity are fluid—and they are—then destination seems at least as important. I'm not talking about a sentimental "sense of place" with its ancestries and traditions and descriptions of landscapes and good things to purchase and eat—that doesn't speak to migration, to *re*-location. Destination is obviously changeable, even arbitrary. What's striking about destination is that it involves a plan, an intention to arrive; but "intention" overstates what I'm talking about, I'm talking about the act of choice, the visible gesture and process of argument.

This leads to destination, this led—for some folks—to locations in Nova Scotia.

When I arrived I set out to visit the sites. The Black Cultural Centre's director, Henry Bishop, had advised me that in Nova Scotia, "We're a rural population." Armed with a black-communities map, my wife Katharine Wright and I went out and got to Lucasville and to Hammonds Plains, both northwest of Halifax, on 9 March. Halifax, I'd discovered, has rather many Anglican churches, their severe angles and austerity and stone building materials making them easy to spot and identify from a distance. But leaving the city and progressing into the country we saw that those were not much in evidence. Instead we came to the variety of structures—tall, squat, reclaimed from other uses, old, newly built—that served the local Baptists who were, from the number of churches, fairly well ensconced. A large part of the black history of Nova Scotia is the history of the Baptist church: the new volume in the popular "Images of Our Past" book series, *Historic Black Nova Scotia*, devotes its second and third chapters ("Baptism by Fire" and "Later Pastors") to Baptist church activities; a sixth chapter politely *others* the non-Baptists with its title, "Pioneering Lay Personalities and Secular Organizations" (Pachai and Bishop iii). It was cold but bright on the day that we drove out to Hammonds Plains. Much of the discourse around blacks in Nova Scotia has mentioned the weather: the Provincial Assembly, e.g., in an 1815 address to the Lieutenant Governor in protest of black emigration, referred to "people unfitted by nature for this Climate" (Grant 24). From my journal:

> On the road to Lucasville we came up behind an older black man, heavyset in a tight brown leather jacket/coat, with a walking stick, walking down the middle of the lane in front of us, his back to us. Stiff-legged, tottering. I flashed on the old man I saw in Newport, on my way to Mr. Giscombe's house.

Newport's a crossroads town in central Jamaica; I had been on my

way to interview a distant relative. ("Trees shaded the way for the
first quarter mile or so, and I saluted an ancient man with a cane
who was walking in the road there, tottery on his bare feet, and he
returned my wave shakily with his free hand" [Giscombe 17].) The
journal continues:

> Something in the gait and the arrogant nonchalance, the tight
> jacket and all, the walking stick. The man in Jamaica had been
> barefoot of course, which won't do in March in Nova Scotia . . .
>
> We came back over the Lucasville Road and went up to
> Pockwock Lake, the Baptist churches continuing, K pointing
> out black people in yards and on porches of the stark houses
> along the road . . .
>
> Got the image: stark houses, empty space between 'em,
> black tottering in the road. Now where's the history?

I had understood my experience that day—though I neither met nor
spoke to anyone—to have been a vision. Stories proceed via images
and this was my first image of black Nova Scotia. The bad effect of
the cold is, I think, overstated, and in any event is stated so often
as to achieve the effect of an unfunny joke, one whose structure
of humor depends on the yoking together of unlikely elements, a
familiar strategy of the race joke. James Baldwin, in "Stranger in
the Village" (his account of his sojourn in a tiny Alpine hamlet):
"Some of the men drink with me and suggest that I learn how to
ski—partly, I gather, because they cannot imagine what I would look
like on skis . . ." (Baldwin 151). I took pains to write it down, my
description of the day (its bright cold, its winter sky, how the light
"bathed" this place, this black and profoundly rural north), and later
shared what I had seen in an interview with David States—a black
Loyalist descendant and amateur genealogist—of Parks Canada,
who spoke to me as part of his work on public educational pro-
grams. He shook his head and told me that Hammonds Plains was
not a Loyalist site but that the people I saw there were the descen-
dants of the War of 1812 refugees.

3.

If Paul Gilroy can locate Crispus Attucks in the welter of history I
wish to locate the black Loyalists who stepped twice out of history.
I do not wish to *fix* them in some particular spot but to speak about
them, to indicate that they are out there. Let me mention Baldwin
again, his "Autobiographical Notes" from *Notes of a Native Son*:

> I know, in any case, that the most crucial time in my own devel-
> opment came when I was forced to recognize that I was a kind
> of bastard of the West; when I followed the line of my past I
> did not find myself in Europe but in Africa. And this meant
> that in some subtle way, in a really profound way, I brought
> to Shakespeare, Bach, Rembrandt, to the stones of Paris, to
> the cathedral at Chartres, and to the Empire State Building, a
> special attitude. These were not really my creations, they did
> not *contain* [my italics] my history; I might search in them in
> vain forever for any reflection of myself. I was an interloper;
> this was not my heritage. At the same time I had no other her-
> itage which I could possibly hope to use—I had certainly been
> unfitted for the jungle or the tribe. I would have to *appropriate*
> [italics mine] these white centuries, I would have to make them
> mine—I would have to accept my special attitude, my special
> place in this scheme—otherwise I would have no place in *any*
> scheme. (Baldwin 10)

If the aforementioned veil can blind, it can also, quite effectively,
contain. ("Leaving, then, the world of the white man, I have stepped
within the Veil . . . ," said Du Bois [Du Bois 3].) These are, of course,
complementary functions.

Identity—national, ethnic—is, at its best, fluid. I would argue
that over the course of the Revolutionary War and in its aftermath
numbers of black Americans—slaves—reinvented themselves
as loyal British subjects, Loyalists. That is, they fabricated a new
and obviously more advantageous national identity. This is, to my

reading, one of the obligations and advantages of the kind of bas-
tardy that Baldwin names: it necessitates the bastard or the bastard
group synthesizing a relationship with power or, more to the point,
being under no illusion about the nature of relationships (or the
fickle nature of power)—belonging is not immutable, heritage is
not immutable. Due to neither leave nor inherit anything but a
continuation of their status as slaves, they *appropriated* the unlikely
mantle of "Loyalist" when the opportunity to do so presented itself.
If the white Loyalist refugees to Nova Scotia were—as described by
Simon Schama—"middling sorts who had backed the wrong horse"
yet who were "accustomed to a decent fashion of life, which usually
included black house servants to wait upon them," (Schama 228)
the black Loyalists arrived in a quite different boat. Or, to maintain
Schama's metaphor, the horse they backed had not won but had
placed.

In 1999, in the pages of *Acadiensis*, Barry Cahill and James
Walker squared off in regard to the historical status of the black
Loyalists. "My purpose in tracing the origins of the Black Loyalist
hypothesis," Cahill wrote, "is to show that it is not only an historical
myth, but also a potentially dangerous one, since the main constitu-
tive element of the myth—Loyalism—was not relevant to fugitive
slaves" (Cahill 78). He goes on: "The Black Loyalist myth helped to
bring Black people into the mainstream of historical scholarship . .
. It was not until the freed Blacks had become Black *Loyalists*—had
joined the club, so to speak—that their historical significance began
to be appreciated. They had to be assimilated" (Cahill 80). His point
is that this assimilation—by granting to early Nova Scotia blacks
the status of Loyalists—is a recent (1970s) "invention of academic
scholars," (Cahill 77) one imposed, if graciously.

Walker counters impressively with a paper trail that pretty
much proves that the black people arriving in Nova Scotia—aside
of course from the slaves of the white Loyalists—had been referred
to by the British as Loyalists; and, as contradiction of Cahill's claim
that "that [as Loyalists] was not how they [blacks] saw themselves,"

(Cahill 80) he quotes a number of petitions authored by black people referring to themselves as Loyalists and claiming the rights that that status should have afforded them (Walker, "Myth, History and Revisionism," 89–91). None of this, of course, contradicts Robin Winks's qualification, referred to above, or my point about reinvention of two paragraphs ago. Of interest and value are Walker's observations that there was no monolithic mindset or demographic for white Loyalists—white people were Loyalists for any number of reasons (Walker, "Myth, History and Revisionism," 98)—and, perhaps especially, that the number of black people who left slavery after Dunmore's 1775 proclamation far exceeded those—potential soldiers—to whom it was addressed. "There was a belief among the slaves," Walker writes, "widely noted at the time and well-documented, that the British would abolish slavery if they won the revolutionary war" (Walker, "Myth, History and Revisionism," 99). This puts us back at Schama's horse race.

And in all this talk I see Walker's emphasis on locating the black Loyalists within the fold of Loyalism writ large, as "full founding members of Maritime society" (Walker, "Myth, History and Revisionism," 105). He complains about Cahill's use of the a-word ("assimilation") as trendy, the bearer of "rhetorical punch in the post-colonial era" (Walker, "Myth, History and Revisionism," 100) and ends his essay by noting that "[t]he heritage of the black Loyalists cannot be dismissed as cultural appropriation or colonization" (Walker, "Myth, History and Revisionism," 105).

But perhaps he's defending the wrong flank from those charges. While he's saying that the *white establishment* didn't steal he's not noticed that black people walked into the designation and made it their own. In spite of Baldwin's above-quoted "confession" (composed in 1952 and widely reprinted since then) this sort of *appropriation* is not expected of us. This connection is the larger point that Barry Cahill's writing leads me to.

And I'm leery about the big tent idea, the generously inclusive gesture, the recourse to "society" as a thing that's *made* with black contributions. Toni Morrison's volume of Harvard lectures, *Playing in the Dark*, warns:

> Whatever popularity the slave narratives had—and they influenced abolitionists and converted anti-abolitionists—the slave's own narrative, while freeing the narrator in many ways, did not destroy the master narrative. The master narrative could make any number of adjustments to keep itself intact. (Morrison 50–51)

The "master narrative," she notes, "spoke *for* Africans and their descendants, or *of* them" (Morrison's italics) but black people were not its makers (Morrison 50). What's the place of black people in Nova Scotia? Black people are obviously central in its history yet I'm struck by how incompletely the sobriquet "black Loyalist" veils the situation, even as it threatens to do so. "Loyal" is a touchy word for black Americans—loyalty to whites has been, over the years, a thing that has been expected of us, and though I realize and acknowledge that in Canada, British North America, the word has other associations, I note that it provides us here with a term for a place that is not incompatible with the myth—the white master narrative—of the English in the province. And, at the same time, it gives blacks a story to own, "a negro section / in the shared past" (Williams 69) as American blacks "own" the stature of slavery. But the story it gives the province's blacks is, in many ways, an *approved* story, a story that exists as part of state memory.

4.

In Paul Gilroy's *Black Atlantic* chapter on Du Bois he evokes the critic Robert Stepto and that man's volume, *Beyond the Veil*. "Stepto offers a perceptive and subtle commentary on *The Souls* and, in a brilliant move, places it in what he sees as the symbolic geographical

projection of African-American rather than American particularity
. . . For Stepto, *The Souls* is a poetics of race and place" (Gilroy 137).

Fair enough but here it's the geographical projection that's inter-
esting to me. Wikipedia: "The plate carrée projection or geographic
projection or equirectangular projection, is a very simple map pro-
jection that has been in use since the earliest days of spherical car-
tography. The name is from the French for 'flat and square.'" The
advantage of geographic projection is that "the entire sphere, includ-
ing the poles, can be represented on a finite-sized map" (Wikipedia.
org).

Race and place on a small map, one human-sized, one that does
not deny the poles, contradictions, excesses, other geographics, and
that insists on black particularity. I don't imagine myself (in the
writing I'll do about Nova Scotia) to be Du Bois, finding and recon-
structing myself anew in Canada[3] partly because Canada occupies a
profoundly different set of places for me in my time than the south
did for Du Bois in his. But I do find myself interested in the issues of
representation. In George Elliott Clarke's collection, *Odysseys Home*,
in a pan of *The Black Atlantic*, he declares: "All narrative pursues an
original identity, and poetry declares it" (Clarke, *Odysseys Home* 83).
This would be in keeping with what Gilroy—evoking Stepto evok-
ing Du Bois—describes as "a frustratingly organic and seamless con-
ception of the culturally specific and spatially mediated linkages [*The
Souls*] establishes between body, place, kinship, and community"
(Gilroy 137). I was surprised to find myself mentioned in *Odysseys
Home*, since I am not an African-Canadian writer. There in the
second chapter, "Contesting a Model Blackness," I am referred to:
"experimental poet, C. S. Giscombe" (Clarke, *Odysseys Home*, 29).

Fair enough. I accept the qualification and the issues of clo-
sure that the qualification—"experimental"—raises. I'm want-
ing to reject, in particular, the categorical closure, the singularity
(national, racial, "English only," etc.) that the U.S. border posits
for us. (Lyn Hejinian: "In the 'open text' . . . all the elements of
the work are maximally excited; here it is because ideas and things

exceed [without deserting] argument that they have taken into the dimension of the work" [Hejinian 43].) Perhaps this is the moment for me to provide a brief narrative, one that pursues a *relation* or series of *references* to identity rather than its source.

I encountered the black Loyalists for the first time while I was on a 1983 vacation trip to Nova Scotia. All my life I'd been going over into Canada, on any excuse, so this had been just another border crossing—we'd come into Yarmouth on the ferry from Maine, I was on vacation from my work as an editor where it was my job, I said often back then, to say No (that is, to decline manuscripts, to repulse writers' attempts to "come in here with us").

Canada's whiteness was a fact I'd been dealing with for a while: in the cities black folks were a presence, albeit a different one (or different ones) from the variety of presences we are here in the U.S., but in Canada in those days I still felt a romantic freedom from the *duties* of blackness—part of these duties was a watchful awareness, a consciousness of what might be behind me as I traveled through unfamiliar towns in the U.S., or across the landscape between towns. "Got your back," we say to one another nowadays. But in Canada— among those whites up there—there was nothing behind me, noth- ing gaining on me. I had no history in Canada—that is, I was no threat, there was no story of animosity or conflict or jealousy or sex- ual (or economic) rage and ownership. I was a casual expatriate that day, shrugging off my nationality at Yarmouth, as I stepped through customs, like it was a raincoat and the day had just turned sunny.

Quite by accident we arrived, a day later, in Shelburne during the bicentennial of the arrival of the Loyalists. 1783 to 1983. People were in period costumes and displays were up in shop windows. We'd not known that the Tories—whom we'd been seriously taught to casually despise as counterrevolutionaries—had come here and had been welcomed as heroes; the day's celebrations were rather unambiguous about the hero status. But the shop-window displays also revealed the British offers of freedom to the slaves and that great numbers of slaves had responded and also come here, black

Tories. In the photographs of local Loyalist descendants I recognized a black man with whom I'd had a casual exchange earlier in the day.

I wrote a bit about it later, a few pages in a book about my family's adventures in western Canada and Jamaica.

> But here was our variousness. Back at home the comforting and familiar black presence in the Revolutionary War was still the famous picture of poor old Crispus Attucks being killed by those bad Redcoats and here I was, 200 Augusts after the fact, on a street corner in Nova Scotia looking at some tacked together displays that casually revealed an alternative history for us, one I'd not dreamed of and had *certainly* never encountered in school; I would have remembered, I would have been paying attention. (Giscombe 240)

In short, this street corner revelation had been, to me, the uncovering of a colossal lie, one perpetrated through omission and de-emphasis. The veil had dropped off.

Toward the end of *The Black Atlantic* Gilroy restates the book's aims: "Dealing equally with the significance of roots and routes, as I proposed in Chapter 1, should undermine the purified appeal of either Africentrism or the Eurocentrism it struggles to answer. This book has been more concerned with the flows, exchanges, and in-between elements that call the very desire to be centered into question" (Gilroy 190).

This is a continuation of an earlier moment in the book when, speaking of black music, he wrote: "Lines between self and other are blurred and special forms of pleasure are created as a result of the meetings and conversations that are established between one fractured, incomplete, and unfinished racial self and others." And later down the page he brings up Ralph Ellison on jazz. Ellison wrote: "Thus because jazz finds its very life in improvisation upon traditional materials, the jazz man must lose his identity even as he finds it . . ." (Gilroy 79).

To the "lost/found" idea of identity and to the idea of the "unfinished racial self" I would offer that Africadia is *not* the finish to the racial story or history of the United States, it's the *continuation* of it; it exceeds the American argument. It's a geographical projection of *closure-denied* in that it foregrounds not outcome but the fact of choice. For U.S. blacks, Nova Scotia is the contradiction to the open-shut story of black America; it offers—like the ocean—the trope of an unassimilable open-endedness.

5.

We traveled some in Nova Scotia during the spring of 2006. My wife is a photographer and has provided for my project some documentation of forms of land and water in the province, the geography associated necessarily with the black Loyalists.

And I went to talks and exhibitions at St. Mary's, Dalhousie, and in town and I interviewed descendants of black Loyalists. I want to talk here about three of those interviews, three of the four that were most substantial and most interesting to me. (The fourth was actually a *series* of interviews with David States and involved issues of families and family knowledge; I want to address the points Mr. States raised for me later, in other writing.)

I spoke with Henry Bishop on 13 March, at the Black Cultural Centre east of Dartmouth. (Dr. Bishop, as mentioned above, is the BCC's director.) I was surprised at how far away it was from the city centers of both Dartmouth and Halifax, only realizing later that it was quite close to the rural black communities of Preston and Cherry Brook. Our talk ranged widely and covered issues of land ownership (a recurring motif) and family, but I came away most impressed with the point that he made to me in response to my questions about the Loyalists. He emphasized—insisted on—the local and indicated that in his experience and observation it was more important to black Nova Scotians to be Nova Scotians than

to be Loyalist descendants and more important to be Africadians
than to be Afro-Canadians (Bishop).

On the way out Dr. Bishop introduced me to Wade Jackson, a
young man at the Centre's reception desk. Mr. Jackson was a his-
tory buff, Dr. Bishop said, and he left us alone to talk. Mr. Jackson
and Dr. Bishop are cousins, it turned out, and both black Loyalist
descendants. I repeated one of my questions about Loyalist identity
to Mr. Jackson and his demeanor changed. I took pains to make
notes on the encounter:

> When I askt about "Loyalist" and forced the point about the
> word—loyal to whom? loyal to the King?—I got the smile: a
> little pained but too wide to be really painful, a little rueful,
> as though I was visiting the site of a very old joke, one of the
> most basic and most definingly racial of jokes, one of the jokes
> that understates and undercuts and weaves through our iden-
> tification *with* and difference *from* and relation *to* the whites.
> It's that what we say's not exactly the truth or not precisely the
> simple truth, not like "the dog ran down the street." "Ahhh, you
> know," he said, and pointed to a picture of Queen Charlotte
> Sophia that was hanging on the wall. "You know about her?"

I did know about her: Queen Charlotte Sophia was the consort of
George III, the King against whom the Americans rebelled in the
eighteenth century. The portrait was a copy of the one by Sir Allan
Ramsey that hangs in the National Portrait Gallery and it reveals her
to be, unmistakably (or, at least, apparently), a fairly light-skinned
person of African descent. I encountered the painting in the 1980s in
J. A. Rogers's miscegenation history *Sex and Race* (Rogers ii). Perhaps
the most loyal-to-the-Crown of all the blacks, she goes unmen-
tioned in Walker's *The Black Loyalists*, Wilson's *The Loyal Blacks*, and
Schama's *Rough Crossings*. But I take the segue to be significant or at
least profoundly interesting—Mr. Jackson's response to my question
was to smile wildly at me in a way that I recognized and make an
oblique response to racial passing (or, perhaps more specifically, to

a person of color widely or publicly regarded as white).

It's tempting to read this, and the encounters recorded below, as having metaphoric relation to passing narratives. Passing is certainly nothing if not an appropriation of another identity. Classically, of course the person passing does it surreptitiously and in the hope or reasonable expectation of not being caught. But much has been written about the gall of passers as well.[4]

Crystal Mulder, another Loyalist descendant, is the director of the North Dartmouth branch of the Halifax Public Library, and I traveled there to speak with her during the week of 20 March. She drew me a map of her family's four corners in Preston and filled in the map with property lines indicating parcels of land and who was destined to get what parcel. People tended to die without wills, she said, and land was handed down that way. I countered that in the States when you die intestate your spouse inherits everything. Only the first $50,000, she said, after that it goes to your kids.

I brought up my spate of Loyalist questions and her face changed: she grimaced but the grimace had the edge of a smile in it. It was not unlike the change in demeanor that I'd encountered two weeks earlier in my interview with Wade Jackson. Ms. Mulder, however, made no reference to Queen Charlotte Sophia. It was about choice, she said, and choosing to support one ideal of freedom over another. Loyalist identity? "It's about the recognition," she said, "of the historical arrival of our people." She went on: "Loyalism protected a class system that is very British and the political system that supported that class system. 'Loyalist,' for black folks," she said, "refers to the time frame. They were loyal only to themselves."

On 10 June I traveled to Shelburne to spend the day with Elizabeth Cromwell, the President of the Black Loyalist Heritage Society. It was my first time in Shelburne since 1983. Ms. Cromwell met me at a local Tim Horton's and I went off with her and with Debra Davis Hill, the society's registrar, in Ms. Cromwell's van. They showed me the old black neighborhood in Shelburne, Bell's Cove (known earlier as Patterson's Division), Ms. Cromwell pointing out the houses in which she and other black Nova Scotians had lived over the years. Corner lots predominated in the tour and she and I agreed that there was something "important" to living on a corner. We traveled out to Birchtown, three miles distant, and she drove me up the old Post Road, an unpaved trace dating back to the eighteenth century. Black Loyalist descendants, she said, had lived on the road until a few years ago.

I noted that Birchtown was a fair distance—two or three miles—from Shelburne and Ms. Cromwell pointed out that this was typical, that black Nova Scotia towns were often some distance—though not too far—from the market towns; as examples she mentioned Halifax and Preston and Digby and Brindleytown. We circled back to the site of the Society's offices, also in Birchtown, where we met Ms. Cromwell's husband, Everett, who'd been doing some work on the buildings. (The Society's headquarters had been the target of a firebombing in April; records had been lost.) Mr. Cromwell joined us and Ms. Cromwell left us to do an errand. Mr. Cromwell and Ms. Hill and I returned to Tim Horton's and we talked there for a while about history and Loyalism. Mr. Cromwell, as mentioned above, is a black Loyalist descendant; Ms. Hill is as well. When I asked why people had stayed here (as opposed to going to Sierra Leone) they responded that it was land that had kept people here. Ms. Hill said, "Land identified them as being free. That was their identity, that was their freedom."

(In the van, earlier, during the Shelburne tour I'd remarked that Crystal Mulder had drawn me a map of Preston, and the response—from Ms. Hill and Ms. Cromwell—had been appreciative laughter. Later I recalled that during both of the occasions that spring when I'd heard George Elliott Clarke speak, he had mentioned—perhaps somewhat self-consciously—that though he lived in Toronto he still owned land in Nova Scotia. Henry Bishop, of course, also had stressed landownership as being a key component in Africadian identity.)

When I asked in Tim Horton's about Loyalist identity I was not surprised to receive a wide, grimacing smile from Ms. Hill. "They were loyal to the promises," she said, and added, "they were no more loyal than the white Loyalists were."

But Everett Cromwell laughed out loud and said, "It was just a title, they had to have some kind of a title."

I asked how they would like me to represent the community to American readers.

"Talk about our strength," said Debra Hill.

Perhaps, for Nova Scotia blacks, Loyalism is the origin story, the supreme fiction. Wallace Stevens: "The final belief is to believe in a fiction, which you know to be a fiction, there being nothing else. The exquisite truth is to know that it is a fiction and that you believe in it willingly" (Stevens 163). My informants in Halifax and Shelburne seemed quite aware of it *as* a fiction. It being a fiction, of course, doesn't mean that it's not a true story in whole or in part. I'm interested by the intersections between Stevens's quite high-church pronouncement on fictions and Clarence Major's slang dictionary's "story" definition: "not exactly a lie but not the truth either; an elaborate form of verbal self-defense; a person's problems or situation, but especially an explanation; philosophy; sense of reality; condition; excuse" (Major 450).

In the States we have slavery, both as a memory (it was actually quite recent: I *remember* when the last slaves—people born into slavery—died) and as a series of public touchstones—notable and profound in its impact among these of course has been *Roots*. It was an event in television history—the first miniseries—and, as important, it gifted black Americans with a television history that was more impressive (in its scope, magnitude, value-as-entertainment, apparent historicity, and compression) than the much more massive, if generally quotidian, television history of whites. Slavery, of course, is and was much more complicated and contradictory and consciousness-changing than, as the advertising slogan goes, "as seen on TV." But here I think that I am a very different sort of interloper than the one Baldwin describes above—partly because of his efforts and those of many other black people, I am much closer to the power of America than I would have been fifty years ago, the time of his "Autobiographical Notes"; I arrived in Nova Scotia as an American—I was and am still qualified by blackness but I'm also a representative (whether I wish it or not) of American power. It's not my place to tell the Africadians what their origin myths are.

NOTES

[1] "I use the term 'Africadian,' a word I have minted from 'Africa' and 'Acadia' (the old name for Nova Scotia and New Brunswick), to denote the black populations of the Maritimes and especially of Nova Scotia. Other appellations—'Afro-Nova Scotian,' 'Black Nova Scotian,' etc.—are unwieldy" (Clarke, *Fire on the Water* 9).

[2] The website mootstormfront.org has been taken down as of this writing. Entering the URL will transport the viewer to a site containing links to stormfront.org. This website—stormfront.org—is one of the most professionally designed and encyclopedic of the neo-Nazi/racist sites on the World Wide Web.

[3] Gilroy wrote: "It becomes a 'cultural immersion ritual' in which Du Bois, the New England black, finds and reconstructs himself anew in the southern black belt" (Gilroy 137).

[4] In an ostentatiously high-wire moment in Nella Larsen's *Passing* in which a light-skinned black woman toys with her racist white husband's ignorance, the novel's main character is overcome with the desire to laugh. "Irene's lips trembled almost uncontrollably, but she made a desperate effort to fight back her disastrous desire to laugh again, and succeeded" (Larsen 40).

ON MOVING TO OAKLAND, ON REREADING ISHMAEL REED

On my way to Oakland I picked up *Blues City* at Doull's in downtown Halifax, May 2006, Nova Scotia itself having a distinguished past in terms of color and exile. The French had been asked to leave and went off way down yonder to become Cajuns but the black people who came twenty years later, who'd already left the new United States, stayed. They prospered, as Angela Carter said. But "late afternoon downtown Oakland"—Oak-town, O-town, the blues city of the title—"still resembles blue-collar Canal Street of New Orleans more than it does Fifth Avenue," in old New York, Ishmael Reed claimed. Here then was guidance: my town-to-be was "a callaloo of cultures." (Most striking though is that *Blues City* itself starts languidly in New York, Buffalo, and—with affection—in North Platte, Nebraska.)

Thirty years earlier I'd bought *Conjure* at Blue Fox Books in Ithaca, NY, another city of arrival and departure. And came to "Neo-HooDoo Manifesto"—the Manifesto does the heavy lifting, reads Jody the Grinder, gave me the talisman with which I later entered New Orleans (i.e., how, the poem says, "'Everybody from New Orleans got that thing,' Louis Armstrong said once"), notes that "Neo-HooDoo has 'seen a lot of things in this old world.'" And starts its chant of saints with Louis Jordan (who sang the query, "Caledonia, Caledonia, what makes your big head so hard?"). And ends with the addendum, two recipes (Gombo Fevi, Gombo File), under the title of "The Neo-HooDoo Aesthetic," asking "Why do I call it 'The Neo-HooDoo Aesthetic'?" and answering, in its own italics, "*The proportions of ingredients used depend on the cook!*" It's a reading strategy, one of the first I encountered! (I was on my way to Oakland, though I was not yet aware of it then.)

In a praise song for Homer's *Odyssey*, *Blues City* wonders why it's not classified with the Koran or the Bible as a work of religion and asks, "what contemporary writer could get away with introducing gods and goddesses to move the plot when stuck?" So this is where I was rowing home to, this bronze Ithaca, "a city where identities blur."

BOLL WEEVILS, COYOTES, AND THE COLOR OF NUISANCE

Histories of "The Boll Weevil Song" tend to lead back to Charlie Patton (1891–1934) and his 1929 recording of "Mississippi Bo Weavil Blues," made under the name Masked Marvel at Paramount's Gennett Studios in Richmond, Indiana. The sobriquet was a Paramount sales ploy—a free record would be awarded to anyone correctly guessing the Masked Marvel's identity. The song has been covered and varied by any number of folks since then—Lead Belly, Woody Guthrie, Bessie Smith, the White Stripes, among many others.

In the lyrics, a farmer and a boll weevil square off about a piece of land and the cotton on it: the farmer catalogues the ways in which he's tried to destroy the weevil, to make the environment uninhabitable for the insect and the insect's offspring (the eggs are laid inside the plants) but the weevil replies that he'll make himself a home-place—that he'll make himself *at home*—no matter what the farmer does. It's a call and response song, a verbal sparring contest.

And there was truth there—the weevil's with us still. Weevils, at maturity, are a scant quarter-inch long but quite capable, in numbers, of laying waste to a cotton crop. A 2003 USDA bulletin, leaning on Carl Sandburg's version of the song for an epigraph, made this unironic observation: "Since its entry into the United States from Mexico in 1892, the insect scientifically known as *Anthonomus grandis* Boheman spread throughout the South, forcing radical economic and social changes in areas that had been almost completely dependent on cotton production. Many experts consider the boll weevil second only to the Civil War as an agent of change in the South." And the insect, like the Civil War, has had different levels of meaning for the black southerners who *worked* the fields than it's had for the white captains of the industry who *owned* the fields. There are lots of ways to configure "home."

I heard the song at ten, in the spring of 1961. Hospitalized for months then, the result of an unlikely injury—a backyard fall—I lived by my radio and learned the words to all the music on the Top Forty, including Brook Benton's "Boll Weevil Song" (which made it to number 2). I was drawn to the spoken interplay, the dialogue—with Benton's smooth, familiar voice taking both parts—and especially to the sung refrain's changes: "Gotta have a home" (in the weevil's strident voice at the beginning) becomes "Ah, you have a home all right, you have a home" (in the farmer's grudging tone) by the end of the record. Reencountering the song in other versions, including Charlie Patton's, in the years after that I liked more and more the complex metaphoric action I'd sensed at ten—man and weevil are both homeless but at odds, profoundly alike and profoundly different. Their places in the song shift, their voices come a little undone—I was ten when I heard it first but I saw it was different than other songs on the radio and I count "The Boll Weevil Song" as being among my early encounters with the stuff of poetry. And, in those later years, I also came to understand the song's wide appeal—worker populations, white and black, were shifted by weevil infestations and signature lines in the lyrics varied interestingly (and were interestingly similar). From an Oklahoma Cooperative Extension publication:

> Now if anyone should ask you
> Who it was that wrote this here song,
> You can say it was just a homeless Farmer
> with ragged britches on,
> Just hunting for a home, yes, hunting for a home.

And this transcription from the "Great Migration" website at the University of Illinois:

An', if anybody should ax you
Who it was dat make dis song,
Jus' tell 'em 'twas a big buck niggah
Wid a paih o' blue duckin's on,
Ain' got no home,
Ain' got no home.

My sister and I were born in Ohio in the 1950s; we were northern
city children. We lived in Dayton, on the West Side—all black
Daytonians in the '50s and '60s lived on the West Side, the neigh-
borhoods on the west side of the Miami River. Our parents had
come from the south but we were distant from the old country and
its traditions. We were a progressive family and this was the post-
war prosperity; we were beyond familiarity with red dirt and cotton
fields. We were Baby Boomers, we were trained to be polite; we
listened to Top Forty radio and went downtown to the library and
the big department stores and we watched the Saturday matinees
with the white children who lived across the Miami, a waterway we
knew we could not cross casually; I mean we knew we had a differ-
ent value—a different *meaning*—in the neighborhoods over there.
But downtown was common ground and in the downtown theaters
I sat through *Bambi, Snow White,* and the loose-limbed jiving crows
of *Dumbo*; watching TV at home, staying with the Disney industry,
I caught the act of ineffectually wicked Br'er Fox and dim-witted
Br'er Bear, seeing only much later their connection to both the
minstrel tradition *and* the animal stories from black folklore. I came
to the animal stories themselves after I was grown, in my thirties;
I was teaching by then in universities and would cover a week or
so of folklore as part of my course in African-American Literature.
I argued in those classes for the primacy of the trickster figure, the
figure often cast as a small animal (a rabbit, say, or a spider) or a
marginal one (a coyote, e.g.). We read beyond Joel Chandler Harris
(whose Uncle Remus stories were an origin point for Disney's *Song*

of the South), we read stories collected by Richard Dorson and published by Langston Hughes; I scandalized my students with "The Signifyin' Monkey." I sent them out to look at graffiti that someone had painted on a paved rail-trail near campus, part of the city's much-publicized Circle Greenway project: "Emerald Necklace? Feels more like an ass-fault choker to me, said Coyote."

Teaching the animal stories made me like and admire them—I fell hard for the stories, for the language I heard and saw there, the language that created them with repetitions and varieties of address. Reading them, I could hear the performance, I could feel the resonance with moments of speech in my own experience with black adults and children (including unguarded moments of my parents' speech). Everything connected—language, race, geography, animals in a variety of roles. And I recalled the farmer's complicated conversation with the bo weavil, the articulation of difference and confrontation that I'd first heard in a black voice at ten, in "a novelty song" on the radio.

Charlie Patton sang and spoke thus:

> Bo weavil left Texas, Lord,
> he bid me "fare ye well," Lordie
> (spoken: Where you goin' now?)
> I'm goin' down the Mississippi, gonna give Louisiana hell,
>   Lordie
> (spoken: How is that, boy?)
> Suck all the blossoms and he leave your hedges square, Lordie
> . . .

But we were far from all that as children and, later, as young professionals in the '80s and '90s, further still—at least in our daily lives. We both left Dayton after high school but have visited frequently over the past forty years, have witnessed the inevitable economic and social changes. There's still an old-money neighborhood in Dayton where black people don't live—though, to be fair, my sister and

I do shop there, when we're in town together, and eat at the fine
restaurants on its main drag, Far Hills Avenue. Our Visa cards are
welcomed and the waitresses are polite. I tend to "read" cities and
locations as though they were poems—ambiguous, contradictory,
riddled with echoes of other poems and other places. You can under-
stand a place, in part, by the kind of animal life it supports (a sen-
timent not original with me). How might *all* a town's populations
work their way into the big poem, the epic, of a particular location?
Or how might the populations resist the poem's definitions or prove
more slippery than the demographic? And how can the sentimental
be avoided?

November 2007 came and the Giscombe children were back in
Dayton for a long weekend. Our parents were old and ill and we were
in town to interview health care providers. One rainy evening, on
the way back from an appointment, I pulled off onto the shoulder
of a new highway so we could examine a piece of roadkill. This was
Ohio Route 49 just below the intersection with Little Richmond
Road, the old way over to faded Indiana; this was the half-rural edge
of the storied West Side, unchanged black Dayton, and my sister and
I piled out to see that I'd been right—it was a coyote, *Canis latrans*,
legs almost broken off, head half-smashed, the fur still beautiful in
the rental car's headlights. They're western animals; I knew they'd
been extending their range east for decades but I'd not known they'd
made it as far as Dayton, as far as the fields and scrubby woods and
culverts between the houses and businesses of the West Side. This
was no trickster figure; Googling "coyote" and "ohio" later I found
that there've been coyotes in Dayton for a while now and that in the
state game laws they're a nuisance animal, an animal with "no closed
season"—you can shoot a nuisance animal at any time. How'd this
guy get here? Let music come up:

> First time I saw Mr. Boll Weevil,
> He wuz on de western plain;

Next time I saw him,
He wuz ridin' on a Memphis train . . .

I've taken pains to locate the coyote among us but there's really no
lesson in any of it, no complicated metaphor; and neither is this a
poem about "swerving" or my heart being ambiguously "fastened to
a dying animal." Location's a jumble of proximities and coincidence.

SONNET TALK

I appreciate the articulate—"coherent verbal form"—but am not terribly interested by it. In university poetry classes I wish—instead?—to put my back into acknowledging the stuff around the poem (around and beyond the impulse and also the sources of impulse), the permissions usage grants us, what knowledge of poetry obligates us to do when we write (what knowledge of culture obligates us to do when we write), etc. And I want, in class (and alone at my desk as well), to be furiously caught up in language—the instabilities, the heft, the fringe elements.

I've recently been teaching two forms, the sonnet and the ghazal. I'll talk here about the former. I'm not terribly interested in sonnets (or ghazals) in terms of my own writing—that is, I've never written a sonnet and probably never will write one. No hostility, no principled stand—I simply have other things to do. But I find the form interesting as a site, as a point of disembarkation for *talking* about that other stuff, for the ongoing work of investigation and experiment. Sonnets can be navigated but the point, in all my classes, is not to get it right but to see how it feels to get involved in it, that and to look at what the poem (or the essay or joke or speech) *does* and at the ways the world presses on it, and at how it presses *back* on the world. We talk about Shakespeare and Donne and Michael Drayton and Shelley; we differentiate the Elizabethan sonnet from the obviously superior Italian sonnet. We consider responses to the form—Ted Berrigan, Edwin Denby, a twenty-four-line sexually explicit sonnet with commentary, both by Molly Peacock, sonnets-it-took-me-a-long-time-to-recognize-as-sonnets by James Wright and Robert Hayden—and I ask my students to look closely, finally, at two stands of sonnets that have been particularly important to me: Gwendolyn Brooks's "Gay Chaps at the Bar" sequence and Bernadette Mayer's book *Sonnets*. The point here

being that both Brooks and Mayer tangle awkwardly and repeatedly
with the form, with the received pattern of lines and syllables and
turns, the daily order of arrival. Of course it's the wrestling that's
important, the labor there, not the form so much. The form allows
us to talk in class about the wrestling; it's a thing, a topic, a place or
placeholder in the never-ending conversation. Like most such places
it has application beyond itself, beyond sonnets and beyond poetry.

Bernadette Mayer said that her sonnets were "brief conclusive
thought" and wondered, "If there are no conclusions why do we
wish for them?"

But before we talk about Brooks and Mayer I start things by
going to the board, chalk and eraser in hand, with thirty-five or forty
minutes left before the end of class. It's a gimmick but I like doing
it. I talk about iambic pentameter and point it out in Shakespeare
or in Drayton's "Since there's no hope, come, let us kiss and part";
and I recite my two favorite iambic pentameter lines—"I hate to
see that evening sun go down" (the beginning of W. C. Handy's
"St. Louis Blues") and "I wish I was an Oscar Meyer wiener." The
latter works as iambic pentameter but *wiener* must be slurred into
a single stressed syllable, a worthwhile task for the voice. I come up
with a first line (most recently, "My love was like a bat that flut-
tered by") and the class writes the sonnet—their choice of Italian
or Elizabethan—in blab-school manner in the time remaining. Let
it—the form—be an arbitrary occasion; let it come to life, mon-
strously, in the moment.

Gwendolyn Brooks wrote, in the first poem in "Gay Chaps" (her
war series, her "souvenir for Staff Sergeant Raymond Brooks and
every other soldier"):

> We knew how to order. Just the dash
> Necessary. The length of gaiety in good taste.
> Whether the raillery should be slightly iced
> And given green, or served up hot and lush.

Because of my life in the academy and my visibility beyond the university I know the complex trap of articulation, the easy praise we get for being "articulate." The oratorical has its place yet I know that this—getting it right or "right"—is what's expected of me. That or to shake things up with surgically precise dance. I ask my students for less than that or more. Or something other.

From my place at the blackboard though I insist on more or less complete sentences that spill over the precipices of rimed line endings, which is to say I gnash and pontificate and cajole them when necessary into using the stuff they learned in school and bending it. I pop a sweat and they sweat too. Much shouting in class, and laughter and more laughter as students argue verbs with one another. This is fieldwork, I don't know where it will end when we start. What we get to is something "that is not mine, but is a made place," and sentence and line we get it done before the end of class.

HARRIET BLOG / POETRY FOUNDATION INTERVIEW (WITH MARK NOWAK)

Mark: There's a wonderful anecdote early in June Jordan's *Soldier: A Poet's Childhood* about waiting as a young child for the arrival of a train, that "moaning in the dark," that "transitory signal from a hidden fire" that "eased its promise into the night." I seem to be reminded of this Jordan passage every time I read your new writings. The acknowledgments section in your new book, *Prairie Style*, concludes: "Portions of this poem were written on Amtrak." And the trains themselves rail their way, so to speak, across the book, particularly in the central (Mid-American?) section, "Inland (. . . poems about Downstate Illinois)," in works like "Fever" and "A Train at Night" and "Afro-Prairie." What is it that keeps bringing you back to those modernist machines that roll along on predetermined tracks?

C.S.: My thanks for your patient reading of my long-winded acknowledgments section. I'd wanted to name Amtrak because my interest in the railroad continues past the romantic images of trains that one sees everywhere, images that the fact of Amtrak is necessarily at odds with. I note of course that Amtrak as a business makes use of (and does spur on) the nostalgia over rail travel—they use it as a selling point. Amtrak wears the mask of some sort of old imagined or imaginary elegance but the mask is rather obviously a tired old mask. The name itself—Amtrak—betrays our worst nominative tendencies: it's one with Kleenex and Miller Lite.

But part of what I like about the railroad is that at core—behind the mask—it's not sentimental; it's a business that's evolved over the last couple of centuries and it still uses the same physical superstructure. The railroad business is continuous. The Rockville Bridge over the Susquehanna at Harrisburg was built in 1902, still used by

155

Amtrak; also in Pennsylvania, the Starrucca Viaduct, over the wide valley of the creek of that name, completed in 1848, still used by the Norfolk Southern; the gorgeous Hell Gate Bridge over the East River, linking Queens and Manhattan, was completed in 1916, still used by Amtrak. Implicit in that list is another thing I like about the railroad—that it's intimately connected to features of land and water, the stuff that is, the stuff that defines. "Geography's irreducible in the world, a fact, opaque," I said once and then, "Railroads describe it."

And all this stuff is profoundly racial as well—railroads divide and define cities. Note that a tenet of urban sociology is the idea of the "natural boundary"—neighborhoods are created by (and their separateness is maintained by) rivers, hills, etc., but also by railroads, hence the phrase, "wrong side of the tracks." So a railroad, in town, is itself a natural boundary or has that value or tends to have that value. I'm typing this in my parents' house on the West Side of Dayton, Ohio, the neighborhood where I grew up, black Dayton—the West Side is and always has been the residential area where the railroads are; the West Side is really several neighborhoods but the tracks and trains brush up against people's houses over here in black Dayton more than anywhere else in town. This is the vista I became familiar with at an early age, this consciousness is a huge part of my railroad sense.

Mark: Architecture (and its relation to home, to location and dislocation)—from Frank Lloyd Wright's "Usonian" designs to Chicago's Robert Taylor Homes—plays an increasingly significant role in your new work. What is it about built place and habitation, particularly in the Midwest that is so much the focus of *Prairie Style*, that allows it to act as both a fulcrum for and metaphor within your poetic practice? And why, as you write in "I-70 between Dayton and East Saint Louis, Westbound Lanes," is property "a measure of elimination"?

C.S.: For me, habitation has, within it, a whole slew of unsaids and relations. There's the cultural value of owning your own home (that familiar phrase); and then there's your house's "real" value, the ever-changing market value—websites'll tell you what your place is worth in US dollars. What can I get for it? Well, that depends (as the real estate truism goes) on location, location, location. It depends on the neighborhood, on the place's proximities and juxtapositions, on its relationship to other human settlement. When you market your house or your apartment you're also marketing that other human settlement—who are you going to see on the street as you disembark from your new address? At this moment—the moment of this question—the issue of marketability places the human and the habitation on the same level.

And—this in response to your concern with "poetic practice"—I'm thinking of poetry as a gift economy; that is, I'm thinking of the worthlessness (conventionally speaking) of poetry as property. This is, I think, a profound strength that poetry has, its off-the-grid existence. Sometimes I hear ambitious people talking about marketing their poems.

Property as "a measure of elimination"? In an apocalyptic dream I wrote down in the 1980s I saw a slogan printed and nailed to a fencepost: "What you own can be taken from you." Or, of course, it can just walk off one day. Intellectual property can give you the slip.

Where do we live? And who is this "we"? What's the range of assumption behind the question? Who's included? Who's excluded? Increasingly I'm finding myself interested in range, in how variation takes place over a geographic space—I'm thinking of populations (human and otherwise) and customs and identifications and, God knows, landscape. Much of the "place" of a middle section of this *Prairie Style* book, the Indianapolis poems, comes from the neighborhood in which I stayed in that city—the Near North Side, with its in-progress gentrification efforts, its influx of whites to the streets of Arts and Crafts houses in which black people live now (or were living in 2000 during my sojourn in Indy). The shape of the range fluctuates and neighborhood—one of the big topics in my head when I look back over *Prairie Style*—speaks to this, I think. I hope.

Mark: I've written earlier here on *Harriet* about what I called a "NAFTA Superhighway Poetics," a poetics of vertical mobility across the continent that is not solely an east-west "American" poetry but a north-south North American (or larger) one. This has certainly been (to me) one of the most engaging and inspiring parts of your own expansion of poetics in books like *Giscome Road* and *Into and Out of Dislocation*, where particularly British Columbia and Jamaica inhabit and in many ways drive the poetics. Perhaps that's part of the challenge you're issuing poets in "Afro-Prairie" when you write, "Everybody wants to be the singer but here's the continent"? Do we need to be singing beyond the nation-state to larger forms, systems, geographies, et al?

C.S.: I read your question and immediately remember two things: one is hearing Michael Manley talk about the rise of multinational corporations, this at a lecture at Cornell early in the 1980s, the first time the shifting nature (or shifting definition) of nation—and its conflation with big business, long the thing that the gangster films, the film noirs, had been metaphor for—had been brought to my attention. The second event was my own travel to Jamaica in the mid-1990s and meeting people there who told me that Michael Manley was a white man, a Jamaican certainly enough, but white (or *and* white). Which had not been my understanding as I watched him in that room in Uris Hall.

I see these two events as reminders to me, or signals of my burgeoning understanding that borders are flexible—national ones as well as racial ones. Or that the flexibility and interesting uncertainty that I'd always understood about race was even bigger than I'd imagined and that nation touched it with a limber finger. What's interesting of course is not the border itself but statements about it, approximations of it, attempts to describe it as well as the way that it's constructed. I'd wanted to "kit-bash" the book some, to stick what America refers to as "our" southern and northern neighbors (and who is this "we"?) into a writing project about the Midwest. And we're back again to that focus on neighborhood.

Mark: Your "prairie," unlike the prairie's construction in much classic literature and contemporary poetry, contains multitudes. One of the "Prairie Style" poems (62), for example, opens with an epigraph from Emma Lou Thornbrough's *The Negro in Indiana* (". . . to designate a person with any discernible amount of Negro blood"), moves across the racialized neighborhood ("it starts because of the neighborhood"), and ends with that marker of Capital, "property." What about the relations between poetry and race and property across the prairie do you want readers to understand or question as they read your new book?

C.S.: I see that poetry, race, property, and geography are not one but form a very ragtag and uncertain army, one with shifting ranks and alliances. What's interesting to me here is that it's possible or even necessary (at least for me) to read each one in the context of the others. This is, of course, not a new thing in the world—when I look back over the book and pause over the poets I quote (Gwendolyn Brooks, William Carlos Williams, Kamau Brathwaite, others) I see the jagged unexpectedness of their work, the big incorporations. I mean here that I see the range and worldliness that their language bangs up against—I address their work with mine. Frank Lloyd Wright's architecture and the Robert Taylor Homes were starting places for me in terms of the book—when I taught in downstate Illinois my black students were eager to let me know that they didn't come from the Robert Taylor Homes. I admired the long lines of Prairie School architecture. But the Robert Taylor Homes is a horizontal project as well and the two things sit in uneasy juxtaposition in my mind.

I note Thornbrough's qualifications alongside her cautious definition work. What does it mean to be black? Well, that varies from place to place. Pit this against NAFTA.

Mark: Finally, toward the end of the book there's a piece titled "Republican National Convention 2000" that seems to have its finger on the "previous" button on the television remote, flipping back and forth between political coverage and *Caligula*. If your moviegoing self could program films to run simultaneously with the 2008 Republican and Democratic conventions, what films would you choose? And why?

C.S.: Watching John McCain on some late-night talk show I found myself thinking of *Young Frankenstein*. McCain's wish to distinguish himself from his dear old O.G., George W. Bush, put me in mind of Gene Wilder correcting people as to the pronunciation of the name—"It's Franken-steen," he would say. And, as the monster, Peter Boyle's all id to Wilder's less-than-completely-in-charge superego; the project of the flick is Wilder trying to teach the monster to at least look reasonable, to put on the ritz.

I work a bit with the Frankenstein myth in the book—maybe that's why it comes so readily to mind here in response to your question about the Republicans. What's more interesting of course is the transformation of "Puttin' on the Ritz" itself—danced marvelously by Wilder and Boyle—from its 1920s minstrel beginnings (see Harry Richman's performance on YouTube) to the 1940s version (the one in the movie) that invites listeners to "Come let's mix where Rockefellers walk with sticks." Minstrelsy's there, the ancestor to American entertainment spectaculars—the rippling flags and dance numbers—and the convention ain't nothin' if it ain't a spectacular.

For the Democrats? The movie on the other channel has to be *Night of the Living Dead*, the 1968 low-budget flick that's so smart and so scary and that is still—in my humble opinion—the best integrated movie of all time. I'm sure you know the plotline—young white brother and sister drive out to central Pennsylvania to put flowers on their father's grave and are set upon by animated corpses desiring to eat them. The woman escapes to a farmhouse and there meets a young black man played by Duane Jones: introduced fifteen minutes into the movie, he fills the screen as the unambiguous and obvious hero, a dashing man in rolled-up sleeves with a plan for survival. Others arrive; much mayhem ensues and there's humor around media coverage of "the epidemic"; and much irony. Through it all Duane Jones strides like a lawyer from Harvard. He's resourceful, eloquent, and did I mention that he's black? On him—in the big world of the movie—the fraught continuation of fraught civilization depends. The living dead of the title gather outside the barricaded farmhouse. Who are they? Choose your metaphor: terrorists, harbingers of environmental catastrophe, hucksters, brain-dead mall rats, gluttons, anti-intellectuals, the homeless. What's happening in the little neighborhood inside the farmhouse? Inside you get the depiction and performance of tremendous argument, not much sex. If you've seen the film, try not to think about the way it ends.

STATEMENT FOR CHARLES ROWELL

The recently published poetry book—*Prairie Style*, 2008—is about the Midwest, where I've lived. The book leans heavily on speech acts, music, the inevitable geography; it's interested in the talk of black and white Midwesterners. By "talk" I mean a number of things— the inclination for speakers to qualify themselves as speakers and the relationship of that to issues in lyric poetry, the racial dialogues of books such as Thornbrough's *The Negro in Indiana*, love talk, Ellison's evocation of "our little palaver," the stretch of argument, the presence of AAVE and its reception as lazy speech, etc.

Talk's different than voice—natural voice, finding one's voice, coming to voice, big voice, etc.—and from whatever icon or vision we make to steady abstraction or buy off what's waiting for us. Thus, a favorite poem in the book, favorite because of its clarity, is "The 1200N Road Going East":

> To me, image is any value in the exchange. Pleasure's accidental. In any event, it's hard to measure and harder still to memo- rize, pleasure. Image stands in. To me, voice is that which gets stuck in the head, effected voice, or inbetween the teeth, the hiss of love. Songs, eating. Whatever love says it's no image, no consequence. This far inland, the erotic's only obvious from a distance. This far inland you need something more sexual than dichotomy.

Here I'm trying to name or, as we sometimes say, *talk about* what image and authenticity might mean or cost; and certainly talk about measure as well—the poems in *Prairie Style* take the shape of prose. County roads in Illinois are largely nameless, numbered instead, hence the poem's title; no allusion or sentiment's attached to the naming of a certain road. One depends on image to express stance or posture, to establish commonality or produce recognition, to collude. I'm interested, in this writing, in the cost of the exchange, "seeing something"—in Kenneth Burke's phrase—"in terms of something else."

In an earlier book I'd written, in response to a memory of my grandfather's funeral,

but all *value* is assigned, is brought in:

still, being the density & mirror both
was what I found confusing—

the fickle layers to endure, the worth standing in

(Frederick Douglass wrote, "We were all ranked together at the valuation.")

And I'm interested too (in this book and in the ones previous and in the prose as well) in the facts of singing and performance, the act beyond the poem, the act's power to intervene. My interest is not in capturing but in the shape of reference itself. Late in *Prairie Style* I take some pleasure in Junior Walker interrupting his song to announce what, in the song, he's going to do next with his saxophone. He stops—or slows, as a train might slow—"What Does It Take (to Win Your Love)" to *talk* to both love interest and listener. He says, "Gonna blow for you" and then, later, "Gonna blow again for you."

ROLLSIGNS / NOTES ON TRANSIT

Of recent importance to me: Juliana Spahr's idea of *joining* (this as it would relate to joinery rather than the way one might agree to accompany an already existing gang and number oneself among them), Kamau Brathwaite's *tidalectics*, and Fiona Templeton's work with cities; and that at Naropa this past summer (2007) we worked up *interruption* as the literary figure for a kind of performance that gets messy, for a trope for acting out (in the vernacular), for being *difficult*, for becoming difficulty itself. (I worked with an amazing group of women and men who named themselves, the performance troupe, the Grammar Sluts.) These things among others.

But my recourse is, again, to the fact of travel, to—more exactly and widely—the traveling public. The surge beyond the self. I can't get around the cultural without recourse to the physical—what the surround is, and how one moves through it, how one might be flush up against it and/or ignorant of it. One what? Travel's "a) mechanical motion, especially reciprocating motion. b) the distance of a mechanical stroke, etc." (*Webster's New World Dictionary*). Travel's some migration in the world.

> Never seen
> a man
> travel more
> sccn more
> lands
> than this poor
> path-
> less harbour-
> less spade

(Brathwaite in *The Arrivants*.)

Travel's a stain, it spreads; you—the city? You, the stain. (Templeton: "The word 'you' is the pronoun of recognition, of reply, of accusation, of balance; beyond the visual, animate, returnable; 'you' assumes and creates relationship.")

* * *

It's the predictable reach of travel that continues to interest me and that I continue to see as a place of exchange—within that predictable's the unfamiliar or the defamiliarizing moment or potential, proximity providing that. Traveling in public on surface transportation is the situation I come to again and again for a poetic that crosses over, for the surge. The way of going for everyone including people without means. The travel's pretty ordinary—getting from A to B and back—but it gets interesting when you mix in the presence of others there to do something ordinary with you, in spite of you, alongside you. A stranger in blood with whom to share a seat, even if he or she doesn't appear until you vacate the conveyance. Negotiations, abandon on the bus, the geography of seating itself, the density of the standees among one's fellow travelers, and, perhaps most disconcerting, every body's similarity—all stalks are the same.

Banal transit, in transit, transitory, transitional, the *Transit Mulatta* blog ("Stories of Race/Gender/Sexuality & Public Transportation in Pluri-Cultural Perspective," transitmulatta. blogspot.com), the several roads that make up the Trans-Canada Highway, MARTA for the Metropolitan Atlanta Rapid Transit Authority but certain people say it means Moving Africans Rapidly Through Atlanta, the crypto-racial of bus and light-rail, where we're going and with whom, "the erotically charged space of the omnibus" (the abstract for Masha Belenky's "From Transit to Transitoire"), mundane travel, rapid transit, Transportes del Norte's "Omnibus de Mexico con mas de 800 destinos en Mexico y EU" (www.gruposenda.com), my current new relation to Bay Area Rapid Transit, its stations—their mix of outside and inside—the closest thing to the

Old World I've seen in America, city transit.

I grew up in a black and white town, Dayton, Ohio, with a very fine citywide system of electric buses that is largely undiminished now, forty years after I left home. The West Side is still black Dayton and the West Side buses are Number 9 (Cincinnati Street), Number 8 (Lakeview / Nicholas Road), Number 4 (Delphos), Number 2 (Home Avenue), and Number 1 (Drexel). But these are crosstown buses—the rollsigns (route number and street) announce the destinations/directions and the rollsigns are changeable. The driver cranks them and this was and has been the *vision*—the driver standing up inside the bus, reaching up to turn the handle above the big windshield, *changing the destination*, going through two or three or several possibilities. Nowadays rollsigns are electric, a display of lights that spells it out; before, they were linen, replaced by treated paper, replaced by the DuPont product Tyvek. The "opposite" was present, is present: the black Number 9 Cincinnati Street bus became the Number 9 Valley Street bus, bound for the Polish neighborhood on the northeast side of Dayton. The Number 1 bus, Drexel (my bus), turned around and became the Number 1 Third Street bus out to the white areas near the Air Force base, out to where East Third Street becomes Airway Road; same bus and driver, different colors of folks in the seats, and the bus bearing the *name* of the "different" neighborhood like a flag through the streets of this one. This is the relationship, the indication of *you*. I'd hate to stop with the idea of place being dichotomy—it's a way to begin the talk of the cross-cultural, not a note to end it on. What I'm looking for, in my own work and in the writing I admire, is something that's often unstable, something beyond "descriptive prowess" crossing the tenets of some static landscape or map, some ethnography.

The bus is not some transparency—the rollsigns are race-/ethnicity-/class-heavy. The bus is, for now, how I say; the bus goes without saying. Interruption still talks up to power.

I went to Belgium in 2003 and followed, on my bicycle, the tramline from Zeebrugge down to Saint-Idesbald, thirty miles or so, on my way to the Paul Delvaux Museum. Coming though Ostende along the tracks I saw that the tram is both invasive—close passages in the narrow streets—and a familiar presence at once and came there to a clearer understanding of Delvaux's paintings of them. He said: "All those images that entered my head at that time remained and I watched the trams in Brussels because the trams were part of the mobile furniture of the streets of Brussels. As important as a house, a monument, a public square, or any other urban element."

MAKING BOOK

(Winners, Losers, Poetry, Anthologies, and the Color Line)

(A talk for a 2007 MLA panel, "Poetry, Race, Aesthetics." With Kandice Chuh, David C. Lloyd, Tyrone Williams; panel chaired by Dorothy Wang)

I'm wanting to identify myself—as speaker on this panel—in terms of a couple of contexts: writer / difficult black poet included in anthologies, editor. Race informs all categories.

My title comes from Sherley Anne Williams's poetry book, *Some One Sweet Angel Chile*. The title figure is Bessie Smith, about whom Williams wrote the book's central section, "Regular Reefer"; she wrote, "I'll make book Bessie did more than just endure." Hear the echo of Faulkner on Dilsey, "They endured." I'll point out or underline the obvious here, in Faulkner's description, that famous lack of agreement between the proper noun and the pronoun. Thadious Davis suggests that it's possible to read that two-word sentence as "a racial epitaph."

But I'm interested this afternoon in the business of anthologies—that kind of "making book"—for any number of reasons. I've been skeptical of the anthology project for many years yet I'll not deny that I first encountered poetry or first began to read it seriously in anthologies in the 1960s; the work I read then, in those books, I have with me still—it's made me, in part, the writer you see before you today at the MLA. I'm thinking here of the various Nortons and thinking more particularly of Donald Allen's *New American Poetry* and Stephen Berg and Robert Mezey's *Naked Poetry*; both of those books were whites-only (excepting of course LeRoi Jones in the Allen anthology). I was reading Langston Hughes before that and James Baldwin, but always in their own volumes; when I encountered Jean

Toomer in 1970 or 1971—maybe one of the two or three great literary events of my early twenties—it was also in his own book, not as part of some compilation. But today I'm interested in looking back some and looking around as well because I'm implicated in this business, as a speaker on this panel, in that I'm *in* a few of the anthologies I'll discuss and, in addition, I'm an editor (though never of an anthology), I've "made book" myself—I've solicited and arranged, I've had that agency/ability to ask for and to pluck from what's out there and contribute to or trouble (in more ways than I have time to detail here) the idea of the canon.

My continuing skepticism comes from my observation that the most exciting or dangerous or excessive work by a writer is most usually not included in the big market anthologies; indeed, the most dangerous, exciting and/or excessive writers also tend to not make it in. Or perhaps it's that in looking at the tables of contents there are few surprises—the usual suspects are almost always there. We complain about omissions—Why isn't Harryette Mullen in the *Norton Postmodern*?—but the complaints are based on pretensions to a familiar stature, or to the familiar way that stature is claimed or constructed. I was lucky enough, as a university student (and as a high school student), to have teachers who understood contradiction and were not afraid of excess and who'd read widely; they prepared me to be skeptical later when I'd see poets whose work I'd studied collected in a book designed for classroom use.

Perhaps my big question on this panel is What does race *do* in anthologies? In the liberal white anthologies it acts to "round out" the "conversation," to make the anthology "inclusive," to make a fact of "diversity." But does it complicate the yakety-yak, does it challenge the tools and structures, the invisible but moneyed empire of white privilege? If, as Toni Morrison suggests, the "best" or "kindest" response to race in conversations is polite silence, the question for us is not how to "break" the silence but how to break the silence *down*. Anything with this much power—the ability to stop speech acts, to render the discourse of smart folks insensible—has got to be really

interesting. Seeing what it's made of—looking deep at the desta-
bilization—is really to the point. More on this later. Cary Nelson:
"[T]he dominant pattern for many years for general anthologies of
American literature has been to seek minority poems that can be
read as affirming the poet's culture but not mounting major chal-
lenges to white readers."

I need to rag some on a book I used for years when I'd teach intro
creative writing classes, X. J. Kennedy's *Introduction to Poetry*. The
book's existed in many different editions, it's now in its twelfth; it
sells for $66, that's paperback. I'd augment it with the usual clutter
of Xeroxes from the small press and, later, web pages. But here's from
the intro to the 1998 edition, the 9th:

> What is it like to be black, a white may wonder? Perhaps
> Langston Hughes, Claude McKay, Gwendolyn Brooks, Rita
> Dove, Dudley Randall, Yusef Komunyakaa, and others have
> something to tell. What is it like to be a woman? A man who
> would learn can read, for a start, Emily Dickinson, Sylvia
> Plath, Anne Sexton, Denise Levertov, Adrienne Rich, Anne
> Bradstreet, Carole Satyamurti, Mona Van Duyn, Sharon Olds,
> and many more.

While proclaiming its own liberal agenda the paragraph announces
that the "normal" subject position of the reader is white and male.
Where is the paragraph that lists writers who discuss "what it's like" to
be white? Or "what it's like" to be a man? And note that race trumps
gender: our Miss Brooks can't tell the normal reader anything about
the womanly art. An Amazon.com reviewer from Seattle complained
that the book "drags out a piece of road-kill by W.B. Yeats (Lake Isle
of Innisfree), follows with a museum-piece by D.H. Lawrence, and
then astoundingly unearths a bland piece by 22-year-old Adrienne
Rich (written before she learned how to set a page on fire and leave
nothing but holy ash behind)." One out of five customers found
the review helpful.

And what does race do in terms of the black anthologies? What's the baseline? How is a race-based literature established? Or what's the range of reference to racial identity?

The editors of the 1940 compilation *The Negro Caravan* (Ulysses Lee, Sterling Brown, Arthur P. Davis) "do not hold that this anthology maintains an even level of literary excellence." They go on: "Literature by Negro authors about Negro experience is a literature in process and like all such literature (including American literature) must be considered as significant, not only because of a body of established masterpieces, but also because of the illumination it sheds upon a social reality." The introduction to the poetry section somewhat snidely refers to the black authors of "correct poems" while praising "the constant experimenter," Langston Hughes. It's an odd introduction, largely historical, largely a survey. It interestingly attributes the failure of second-wave black poetry—that it "suffered from too great decorousness"—to "the strain that colour put upon the educated poets of the day. They had to be living proofs that the race was capable of culture." And the introduction concludes on a complex note—that if black poets "learn craftsmanship from the best poetry of the past and present without slavish imitation, if they write with sincerity and understanding and passion, American poetry will be the better for them." That is, it gestures toward an unpromised inclusion but also echoes the close of Hughes's "Racial Mountain" essay in which he shrugs off possible complaints from white people and from black people too. The book itself—*The Negro Caravan*—is quite interesting because of the critical stance of its introductions—that is, the emphasis on process and experiment and its polite eschewing of the dictatorship of masterpieces—but also because it contains work that I don't see reproduced elsewhere, meaning since then.

This is now. At school, for the last several years, students have been required to take a certain number of hours of diversity-geared classes. A multicultural industry has emerged to "support" that. More full disclosure: I'm a university professor and teach courses that count toward this requirement and courses that do not—but even in the courses that do not, every month is still February, Black History Month year-round. As such, I'm marketed to, I get the junk mail from publishers and the free copies that are careful, these days, to address the multicultural presence in the national curriculum. I see a lot that interests me but I'm at the point where I think *most* things are interesting. I don't see much I *like*. Now recently, for the past dozen or so years, I've found myself grouped with "innovative (or 'difficult') African-American writers"; I've not resisted this and in fact have taken great sustenance from it, from my friendships with any number of people also so categorized, among whom is Harryette Mullen. Some years ago I put together a Special Focus for *American Book Review*, titled "Maroons: Postmodernist Black Poetry." It was a group of statements from "difficult" black writers, written for the occasion. This is from Harryette Mullen's:

> "Formally innovative minority poets," when visible at all, are not likely to be perceived either as typical of a racial/ethnic group, or as representative of an aesthetic movement. Their unaccountable existence therefore strains the seams of the critical narratives necessary to make them (individually and collectively) comprehensible, and thus teachable and market-able. In each generation, the erasure of the anomalous black writer abets the construction of a continuous, internally con-sistent tradition, while at the same time it deprives the idio-syncratic minority artist a history, compelling her to struggle even harder to construct a cultural context out of her own racial individuality.

I want to use this as a point of departure to talk a bit about the big money anthologies, the ones that end up marketed widely. Alan Golding puts this in historical terms in his book about canonicity, *From Outlaw to Classic*; his project was to write about the context that moves a piece of work—or a writer's output or a group of writ-ers—from his first category to his second. Writing about *Origin* magazine he asks what it means that Mr. Corman's journal has been accorded the "status of the 'best' or 'most influential' of the postwar period?" Answering himself next sentence: "It means that the marginal has become canonized, via critical claims for that margin's centrality in a certain understanding of recent literary history."

What has been more marginal than African-American literature? My memories of going to school in the '60s and '70s are not really *ancient* memories—I still have *clothes* I wore back then and still, occasionally, wear them. But in my career as an undergraduate English major I only once encountered a book by a non-white author (Richard Wright's *Eight Men* in a very forward-looking freshman comp course that had as it topic existentialism) in my classes outside the department's one African-American literature course. But this is now, and we have a few major anthologies, two of which are published under the imprints of Norton and Oxford, names that are familiar to generations of English majors. The problematic action that anthologies take—especially anthologies published by the big houses—is to canonize that marginal, to move it to the center, to either put a suit on it or to raise the value of its Walmart jeans to a kind of chic, a variety of exoticism, what difficult black poet Wanda Coleman calls being nigguh of the month. In Harryette Mullen's term, it's made "teachable and marketable." As what and to whom?

When the *Norton Anthology of African-American Literature* came out in 1997 I edited another special focus for *ABR*. Gerald Early, rising to the complexity of the moment, said that "what we have, in this volume, is the extraordinary instance of a book that pretends to be high-brow, middle-brow, and no-brow simultaneously"; he gestured toward the elitism and exclusivity but, later in his review, he conceded that "as anthologies go, this is a very good one," and commends the section editors. My publisher John O'Brien dangerously mixed his metaphors: the anthology, he wrote, "continues Norton's fine and impeccable tradition of missing the boat by a country mile." He complains of the exclusivity and, as Gerald Early did, named writers not included (including your speaker). But difficult black poet Erica Hunt broke that "exclusive" project down some, also evoking—as Mullen did—*erasure*. She wrote:

> If the canon of American literature has served mainly to
> exclude, silence, or erase the full chorus of literary practice,
> the many cross influences, the many independent discoveries,
> the many formative influences coming from the non-dominant
> culture, why would we, as Black people, adopt this form? Is the
> response to canon making more canon making?

And she concludes her piece with the *OED*'s fifteen definitions of
"canon," from "A rule, or decree of the church, especially a rule
of the ecclesiastical council" (that's number one) to number fif-
teen, "Monument." So see how neatly I've circled us back to that
Faulkner, to "They endured," to another "racial epitaph."

The *Oxford Anthology of African-American Poetry*, which came
out last year, continues the tradition of the Norton. Edited by
Arnold Rampersad, it's dedicated to Nellie Y. McKay, one of the
two key Norton editors, who died in 2006, and features a blurb on
the cover by Henry Louis Gates, the other key Norton editor, who
calls it "a major contribution to American poetry as a whole," which
echoes the sentiment at the close of *The Negro Caravan*'s poetry
introduction. Neither Harryette Mullen nor I are in the Norton but
we are both in the Oxford. The book's broken into sections—"ar-
ranged by themes"—and my poem, "(the recent past)," is in the
section titled "The Rocking Loom of History"; it's a poem having
to do with Birmingham and it references the Scottsboro Boys. My
thought had been that it was a poem about ambiguous slogans and
varieties of public description informed by racial ambivalence, but
there's no section that goes by that name. Still, I'm on the facing page
to the beginning of Robert Hayden's "Middle Passage," an obviously
and undeniably great poem, and am awed to find myself there. But in
the introduction Arnold Rampersad posits and returns a few times to
the idea of cultural truth. The black poet, he says, must "be prepared
to risk even banality to arrive at truths that are peculiar to his or her
culture"; or, later, in reference to music, "the language of the blues
was first identified by gifted writers . . . as speaking cultural truth

in ways that often put the typical black poet to shame." Harryette Mullen's poetry books are legion and inventive and full of pleasures and, yes, difficult; elsewhere in my "Maroons" gathering she wrote, "I think of my first book, *Tree Tall Woman*, as more a derivation and celebration of my mother's (spoken) voice than as the discovery of 'my own voice' as a writer. In poetry I have no voice, only text. I like it that way." Yet it's her early blues-inflected work—six of her eight poems—that the Oxford emphasizes.

Pleased as I am to be part of the show (and aware as I am that my Scottsboro Boys is different in any number of ways from Allen Ginsberg's) I can't help but hear the claim for authenticity that the introduction makes as a cousin to the creepily erotic question—"What's it like?"—that Kennedy and Gioia ask in their book.

In another book that came out last year, Aldon Nielsen and Lauri Ramey's *Every Goodbye Ain't Gone*, subtitled *An Anthology of Innovative Poetry by African Americans*, the idea of authenticity is usefully troubled:

> For [Calvin] Hernton and others, the search for an authentic voice as an African-American poet included being aware of the developments of modernism and its implications for black culture. In fact, these influences are embraced and insisted on by many African-American poetic innovators of the era, in sharp contrast with the image of rather inward-looking cultural isolation sometimes implied by the canon.

But in all this I identify as a writer. Know I make no complaint here. I'm here to make observations, to describe what I see the terrain as being, how my reading strategy breaks this down, how race—in this case blackness—is valued and judged in public, how it's displayed not by those of us who write from within it but by the industry. As an editor these days I'm oxymoronic, I'm looking for ways to exclude less, to open things up more.

I want to close up by revisiting the Norton, by glancing briefly at something else Gerald Early said in his response to the book's publication: that the career of Henry Louis Gates—whom Early characterizes as "an extraordinary man"—"is the expression of the needs of both blacks and whites to have someone like him who can authorize and legitimate . . . black culture." Fair enough on all counts and I would be remiss if I did not pause here and acknowledge that I know of no one who works harder and more effectively and is more generous than Skip Gates. But I can't help contrasting Early's appraisal with James Baldwin's observation of forty or so years earlier that he—speaking for all of us—was "a bastard of the west," black and marginal, uncentered. The desire for legitimacy was useless. I think of this as well when I reread difficult black poet John Keene's contribution to "Maroons," a piece of prose that continues the conversation of Harryette Mullen:

> I do not see my position of marginality as a negative thing, however. From a marginal position, from a place at the edges of the mainstream's arena, I—and all other marginals—am able to participate in the destabilization of boundaries, of categories (racial, sexual, class), to upset language in its official capacities.

This is the outlaw work—destabilization—that I've always thought poetry was supposed to be doing.

FIELD TRIPS

I teach creative writing and have done so for many years. My work as a poet has afforded me a career in the university. The question, again and again, is what am I doing and why? I have little interest in models for "successful" stories and poems. But I like field trips.

My thought these days is that the location—the destination, say—matters less than the motion, the motion out in public.

To go out in public is to go out big into open-endedness, without seeking resolution. "How dull it is to pause, to make an end," says Ulysses in the poem. The deal is to act this out—the unending discovery or series of discoveries that poetry is—out in the field. Out there, "visions" come upon one; Robert Creeley said, "Form is what happens," which is also still just as true. Or one comes upon the vision or into form itself en route because that's where and how I'm arguing it happens—with the mind opened/receptive, made so by the process of *being* en route, that's what the field opens from. Being en route is itself the topic—the uncertainty of the relation of the map to the territory, proximities, unsuccessful aims or plans, jammin'. It's gonna take a lotta love, and much failure. You go out to look at something and if you're lucky and loose and attentive something else happens. I like field trips because on the trip the field slips, shifts, the joke—*intention*—falls away.

In school we read this and that and yammer about it—Bashō, Tess Slesinger, Gwendolyn Brooks, Joseph Conrad, Sei Shōnagon in recent memory, people dead before I was born for the most part though I did meet Miss Brooks—and we go out, based more perhaps on the *shape* of the reading than on the reading's particulars—to Harlem, to Alphabet City, to Yosemite, and up the Strait of Carquinez (in recent memory), to places *lousy* with possibility. We read Margaret Atwood's *Surfacing*, the narrator therein describing lakes and portages, the journey itself to the place in the landscape

where something—holy, damning, saving, "the truth," sexual—
might happen or might not happen. (So we'll leave together for the
territory but there's no promise stated or implied—I might love you
but I can't promise you a vision to complete the field trip, to bring
the strands together. Field trip's not how to construct some image.
You never know.)

I like field trips. Bus waiting which *will* take you there and will
likely bring you back. Field trip's getting to see beyond genre, getting
to *go* beyond—never sure how the trip's going to end, that's why
they sign waivers. I'm interested in alternatives to the ways of telling
that we're stuck with, ways culture sticks us with thinking about
stuff. Amiri Baraka said that thinking is much more important than
writing, that even a stupid man knows he's more important than his
poems. Perhaps this is obvious by now, fifty years later—going out
to the edge and then on beyond that has always seemed to me key,
one of the best jobs of poetry. Go there on a bus, which is to say go
there in public—let 'em see you. I teach the essay, most raucous of
the well-known prose forms, most sexual, which is to say most frank
and basic, most prone to experiment, most incomplete and, because
of that, closest to poetry—now, essay's a verb, y'all *essay*. Phillip
Lopate wrote that the thing about the personal essay is its intimacy.
I like Phillip Lopate but I don't *want* to be intimate with you all or
any sailor, at least not all the time. Elements of poetry—language
as topic, its opacity and juxtapositions, its failures and samplings,
etc.—are themselves useful for troubling ideas of the "intimacy" of
literature. Intimacy's well-known, intimacy's a problem; it means
you know what you're going to get and it might be good but it's
never that surprising. Maybe that's why everybody's supposed to be
so scared of it. In "the folk-tale stratum of the Greek epic" (which
is to say pre-*Odyssey*), is "the case of the sailor who is told to put his
oar on his shoulder and march on until he comes to a land where
they say that it is a baker's peel." Ride the bus out to where you see
things you don't understand.

The Far Field, within which is Roethke's description, "the long journey out of the self"; *The Opening of the Field*; "Composition by Field." Clarence Major's dictionary on "come wind"—that the wind was "often depended on to carry the voice across the distance of a field."

The best field trips are uncomfortable but obviously sexy if you're willing to be loose about what sexual means, to understand that it's not just being able to do intimacy well—you're pressed up against something that you can't predict. Ulysses again: "I am a part of all that I have met." A part of, apart from. Oh mariners!

ON A LINE BY WILLIE MCTELL

Start with railroad music, start with "Statesboro Blues" because it claims southeast Georgia as its stage, because specificity takes its listener to something else. Willie McTell sang, in 1928,

> Big 80 left Savannah—
> Lord an' did not stop—
> You oughta saw that colored fireman—
> When he got them boilers hot!

No narrative to the song—about traveling, about sexual possibility, about the colors of race, about the ambiguous hand-downs of parents. Probably the Midland Railway, the old line over the fifty miles from Savannah to Statesboro; probably a reference to the "massive" 80-inch driving wheels on some powerful classes of steam locomotives.

There's beauty to the railroad, this is given; the railroad's a received form—its "aspects and indications" regarding semaphores, its yard limits, its code of horn signals, the certain ways *movement* is permitted and, within that permission, restricted. In central Pennsylvania, in the first years of the new century, I trained as a brakeman using the NORAC rulebook and later became a petty railroad bureaucrat and worked with people in the industry and the regulatory agencies. Along with others I ran a tourist railroad, centered in Bellefonte, PA, and some of the fellows joked that we were playing train when we went out on the line, but the equipment was real and, because of that, "unforgiving"; and our operation was, like everyone's, governed by rules. We traversed the superstructure, the General Railroad System of North America, the big map that shows the tracks to be in fact all connected, from Hay River to Savannah and Miami and, via Laredo, down to Lázaro Cárdenas and

Veracruz and down east to Bangor and out west to Coos Bay and Prince Rupert; including the Bellefonte Branch and the sixty miles of ribbon rail we shared with freight traffic—coal trains—from Lock Haven to Tyrone.

No firemen on our runs. As brakeman I would swing off to line switches, flag crossings, crank on (and release) the handbrake, set and remove the chocks, conduct the air test. The issue of railroad firemen is complex—the position survived the mid-century conversion of locomotive power from steam (with its fireboxes that, as we would say in Pennsylvania, "needed stoked") to diesel, but by then the pool of firemen, through a series of labor agreements, had been limited to "promotable men." A. Philip Randolph and others fought this in public, with mixed success. There were black brakemen but, as *Time* magazine said, in a piece about Mr. Randolph's fight in 1943, "Almost the oldest tradition in Southern railroading is the Negro fireman." Postwar railroad hirings of black firemen and brakemen are documented in brief articles, often with pictures, in *Jet*. So wasn't I the colored brakeman? Yes, but usage and familiarity are what define and govern—stake out—our positions; fireman was the *storied* job available in engine service, what *Time* described as "the best paid, most aristocratic job a Negro can aspire to in the South." "Promotable men" were white men—one rose from brakeman or fireman to engineer or conductor—and my experience of engine crews is that they are still white, with obvious exceptions, and male (with obvious exceptions); I've seen exactly four black engineers since I began keeping score in 1962 or 1963 or 1964. Engineer's on the right side of the cab, head-end brakeman on the left. As brakeman I would converse with the engineer about track conditions directly ahead—we'd agree that the automatic crossing protection (flashing lights) was working, that switches were lined correctly, etc. I'd watch for foot traffic, kids playing on the railroad, I'd watch for hunters, for people in cars. Much there involved in getting those boilers hot. Why *should* you have seen that colored fireman? Showed his color (but that usually means something else).

The adjective, "colored," for emphasis in the song but it was also a cultural reference, casually made, not an intensifier at all but a *casual* statement of the underpinning of the whole structure of everything in the United States. As a colored *brakeman* in 2003 I was so anomalous I may as well have been white. But I wasn't.

Later I applied to be an engineer and had my eyes and hearing checked and allowed the national inquiry into my forty-year driving record. My student engineer license came in the mail, signed by the superintendent of our operating partner. Months before, I'd made it through his rules class, an all-morning event, and passed the written exam. In my other life then—those years in that place—I was a member of the faculty at Penn State, one town over in State College. But this was Bellefonte, the county seat. One day, as we were taking a half-full train up to Pleasant Gap, PA, my engineer—Steve, the man with whom I'd been paired when I commenced my training—said, "You run it for a while," and I did.

The horn was a problem. It was a piece of rope that hung straight down next to the windshield. Signaling the intention to move forward (two short blasts) or to back up (three short blasts) was fine but the familiar signal for grade crossings was more complicated to execute—as every schoolchild knows it's two long blasts, a short, and another long and "is to be prolonged or repeated until engine or train is on the crossing, or, where multiple crossings are involved, until the last crossing is occupied." The problem was that the engineer should take the equipment through such with his hand on the brake. Fair enough but a childhood accident cost me my left arm some decades ago and it's been a series of prosthetic devices ever since—they've worked well but the horn was a problem. There was the likelihood of slippage if I used my steel hook to grasp the brass brake lever; and if I kept my right hand on the brake the dangling, dancing rope was hard to pluck, with the hook, from out of the air. So I went to Home Depot one morning before reporting for my shift and bought an S-clip and a length of new rope and—with the help of a young man, Timmy, who helped out in general—extended the cord. That is, Timmy and I added a loop, a long down-hanging U across the top quadrant of the windshield, an easier target for my hook—gross movement skills as opposed to fine movement skills, less difficult to pull on and make a joyous noise with, easier for me to pipe wildly down the valleys. Two dollars' worth of parts. "Now we're ADA compliant," said Steve.

Is this disability? My mechanical-man self ensconced in another machine moving across the surface of earth. My cyborg, my amputee, my centaur, my rolling man. *Type of the modern! emblem of motion and power! pulse of the continent!* Cyborg? The dictionary embedded in my MacBook Pro says: "fictional or hypothetical person whose physical abilities are extended beyond normal human limitations by mechanical elements built into the body." My hypothetical self, typically irritable. In a review of a Stephen King novel, *Duma Key*, the reviewer says, "King neatly figures the tropes of dismemberment." But it's only irritation, my response to the tropes (and to neatness); only dismemberment. We on the railroad provided a service, transportation between Bellefonte and Tyrone (or Lemont or Port Matilda or Pleasant Gap), train service; we carried or hauled instances of the body, as ticket holders might be described or configured from afar, while, over the same route, our operating partner carried limestone and I came to understand that what was in the *back* of the train being hauled made no difference to the *vector* of the train, which is what I endeavored to become or at least merge with. We sold our service, including my labor at the throttle or my labor on the ground at trackside. A ragtag gang of white kids stared once at Milesburg as I waited for a coal train to clear the next block before throwing the switch so we could take a full load of paying customers to a restaurant thirty miles away in Tyrone, PA and one of them said, finally and definitively and loud enough for me to hear and not irreverently, "Candyman." Is this disability? Undying famous black monster of filmland Tony Todd with a hook for one hand—a monster is something else. "Specifically, an animal or plant departing greatly from the usual type, as by having too many limbs."

How far is it from too many limbs to not enough? And what are "normal human limitations"? And what did he *do* to white costar Virginia Madsen? Did he dis-member her with his hook? (In the movie he asked her, "Do you fear the pain or what is beyond?" "Both," she replies. "The pain, I can assure you, will be exquisite," Candyman says.) The movie, based on familiar, intersecting urban legends and set in Chicago—in storied Cabrini-Green—came out in 1992. I lost the arm in 1961—normal human limitation would have me get by with the one and people do but I have always had decent insurance, a middle-class shield, so come equipped with high-end metal and plastic and fabric devices to let me cook and drive and get dressed and frame doorways, suspend my weight over a lover's body, bicycle to work; and operate trains. The idea one comes across is that phantom pain is the body's attempt to *re-member* itself and I find the idea precious and tedious both. On the railroad I extended myself beyond the normal into the fictional, the synthetic, without resolution. No Garden of Eden for me, baby; no circling back.

The railroad's centerless (as Alan Gilbert has suggested) which is how it gives off beauty. And it describes the geography it traverses. We'd leave Bellefonte and creep along Spring Creek to the junction with the main at Milesburg. There we'd radio the Altoona East dispatcher in Pittsburgh for Form D clearance to occupy the track; when that came, the brakeman would get off and throw the switch. I remember how it felt to move the train onto the main line and stop so the brakeman could re-line the switch and get back on. The main was continuously welded—ribbon rail—and we'd sail down the valley at thirty miles an hour, through Unionville, Julian, Port Matilda, through the country between those places, the horn blaring as I took us over the highway crossings.

Willie McTell was known as Blind Willie McTell. From the *New Georgia Encyclopedia*: "As a person faced with a physical disability and social inequities, he expressed in his music a strong confidence in dealing with the everyday world." (On the radio as I was writing this—on March 24th 2011—the host of the *Writer's Almanac* announced the birthday of John Wesley Powell and, not mentioning the man's missing arm, that "he and his companions were the first white people to navigate the Grand Canyon Gorge"—Mr. Powell was a promotable man.) There's an urban legend, apparently from Ohio, about a one-armed brakemen with a hook but it's not one of the famous urban legends (in spite of or perhaps because of the heightened possibility of actual brakemen losing real limbs to unforgiving equipment) and is barely a ripple in the big legend-family of hook-handed bogeymen that mostly has to do with lovers' lane jitters and "the natural dread of the handicapped"; the *Candyman* movie pushed the sex that was always there in the campfire stories and complicated it with "the instinctive dread of Negroes." Willie McTell's blindness complicates the situation of his song, his telling the listeners that they shoulda *saw* that colored fireman.

My interest in the railroad goes back to childhood—the everyday world was full of trains and references to them as instruments of travel and as places of employment; trains covered distance, trains were sexual. My railroad career was short—2002 until I left Bellefonte for a faculty job at the University of California in 2007. I saw my first black engineer in 1984 or 1985 in upstate New York and saw the second two in Illinois in the 1990s. The fourth black engineer I saw was myself in the narrow cloudy mirror in the restroom of the Bellefonte train station where I'd change into my coveralls.

No descriptive word or phrase for what I was on the train, no casual assignment. There's no tradition, aristocratic or otherwise, of one-armed brakemen—aside from the bigger one the children in Milesburg understood—or colored engineers. Nor was I a singer no matter how much I love the song; on the railroad I was something else.

BACK BURNER

From one of the Nick Adams stories, "The Killers":

> "Hey, bright boy," Max said to Nick. "You go around on the other side of the counter with your boy friend."
> "What's the idea?" Nick asked.
> "There isn't any idea."
> "You better go around, bright boy," Al said. Nick went around behind the counter.
> "What's the idea?" George asked.
> "None of your damned business," Al said. "Who's out in the kitchen?"
> "The nigger."
> "What do you mean the nigger?"
> "The nigger that cooks."

George Washington's chef Hercules, a slave, made his escape on his owner's sixty-fifth birthday. George Washington Parke Custis, the General's step-grandson, remembered him thus:

> The chief cook would have been termed in modern parlance, a celebrated artiste. He was named Hercules, and familiarly termed Uncle Harkless. Trained in the mysteries of his part from early youth, and in the palmy days of Virginia, when her thousand chimneys smoked to indicate the generous hospitality that reigned throughout the whole length and breadth of her wide domain, Uncle Harkless was, at the period of the first presidency, as highly accomplished a proficient in the culinary arts as could be found in the United States. He was a dark-brown man, little, if any above the usual size, yet possessed of such great muscular power as to entitle him to be compared with his namesake of fabulous history.

John Adams owned no slaves but his cousin Samuel—after whom the popular twenty-first-century beer is named—was given, as a gift, a slave named Surrey; apparently, being opposed to the institution, he freed her upon receipt but she stayed on for many years as cook for the family. James Hemings—Sally Hemings's brother—cooked for Thomas Jefferson and traveled with him to Paris when Jefferson was Minister to France but petitioned Jefferson for his freedom, which Jefferson granted after he, Hemings, had taught his brother Peter to cook French food. Later, James Hemings declined the offer to be Jefferson's chef in the White House.

Other presidents didn't care for French cuisine. James K. Polk had his slave cook sent in from the plantation in Tennessee and Benjamin Harrison imported Dolly Johnson from Indianapolis, both cooks in replacement of French chefs. Mary Campbell cooked for Franklin Roosevelt's mother and when old Mrs. Roosevelt died the president brought her—Mary Campbell—down from Hyde Park and moved her into the White House. Vietta Garr cooked for the Trumans. John and Delores Moaney both cooked for the Eisenhowers; during the war John Moaney, in addition to his duties as cook and waiter, was also in charge of General Eisenhower's Scottie dogs, Caacie and Telek. (But nobody black has ever been chief of the White House kitchen, not even now, never the Executive Chef— black people were the cooks for the family, intimate that way, physically so if you think about intimacy for a few seconds and how it extends like a stockinged or bare foot under the table.) Hugh Sidey's book on the Kennedy White House notes the return of French cooking—"The entire country was distracted when the Kennedys looked for a new cook. Filipino Pedro Udo had been fine for Ike, but Jackie had other ideas. She installed French chef René Verdon as master of the White House kitchen." But LBJ "summoned" Zephyr Wright from Texas to prepare meals for the Johnson family, though René Verdon stayed on as Executive Chef. The Nixons replaced him with another white man, Henry Haller, who "permitted the Johnsons' 'woman cook' (Mrs. Zephyr Wright) to teach him

Texas-style cooking." My survey is casual, downloaded from the Internet, incomplete and superficial, if fairly easy to locate.

2.

Or start again with railroad music. "I've Been Working on the Railroad" is a folk song: a piece of various origin, it surfaced at the turn of the twentieth century and, as the century went on, changed in that a second part—in which the tempo speeds up—became attached to it. Nowadays, after lines having to do with laboring "all the livelong day," lines that lead up to the somewhat mysterious request of "Dinah won't you blow your horn," children sing,

> Someone's in the kitchen with Dinah,
> Someone's in the kitchen I know,
> Someone's in the kitchen with Dinah,
> Strummin' on the old banjo.

The first part of the song, a variation on "The Levee Song," was sung by black and Irish railroad workers in the nineteenth century; the second part is a survival from minstrelsy, the signature American form. In the antebellum days, blacked-up for an "Ethiopian" bedroom farce, white men would sing,

> Oh, somebody's in de house wid Dinah,
> Somebody in de house, I know,
> Somebody's in de house wid Dinah,
> A-playin' on de old Banjo.

Nowadays the intricate licensing that the hijinks of Mistah Bones and Tambo gave to young America's libido is faded from any kind of active public memory; a vague nostalgia's in its place. Dinah's in the kitchen where she should be, doing the work she's supposed to be doing, day after all the livelong day. It's work anybody can do but if race is socially constructed—and every schoolboy knows nowadays to say that it is—race has still got its kitchens.

Now, it's 2012 and my job at home has been to be cook in good times and bad. As for me and my house I run the kitchen—my wok, my skillets, my ability with sauces and marinades. "If you can read you can cook," a woman told me when I rented a room with "kitchen privileges" from her in Boston thirty years ago; conventional wisdom but I heard it first from her. I can read and I can also imagine and arrange and remember and plan and repeat and vary and interrupt. I can map meals for a week. I can cook right through disaster.

A history of cooking? Taken shopping at an early age by my mother on the West Side of Dayton, Ohio—black Dayton—I came to have preferences among the chain supermarkets (Kroger still survives) but came also to value neighborhood groceries with their wood floors and ancient coolers: all were stations of the elemental, places where one went to get supplies for survival, and all were obviously profound places because of that. As I've said elsewhere, we were city people, removed from the land, and did not raise our own food so the grocery stores stood in for the racial acts of hunting and gathering. Sent alone and on foot with money to purchase, say, a loaf of bread from Mr. Sherer's Ice Cream Store I understood myself to be, at twelve, on an errand of basic consequence. When I left home in the 1960s and went east to Albany, NY, I found the upstate chains and later, when I came to Ithaca, the co-ops and farmers' markets and the natural food emporiums. But I always liked best the hustle and bustle of the chains, because their prices attracted people from a broad spectrum—noisy, various. A case in point here is that, in Ithaca, Tops and Wegmans sit side by side, both open 24 hours—big stores with big parking lots, they mark the beginning of Ithaca's strip, the mile of ragtag commerce that commences at the place where the Elmira Road crosses Six Mile Creek. (Tops is now a property of Morgan Stanley Private Equity; its diamond logo represents a spinning top. Wegmans is still owned by the Wegman family.) We lived at 402 N. Titus in a house that faced Six Mile Creek, upstream from the Elmira Road—to get to Wegmans, which I had found to be the superior grocery, my daughter and I would cross the footbridge over the water, skirt the housing projects, and return the same way with our purchases. She was three and we sang the "Bamboo" song, which has to do with home being across the river, when the house on Titus came into view.

History of cooking. Two years before our excursions to Wegmans, Madeline and I would go together—she in the backpack—to shop the Covered Market in Oxford, where we lived then. Cheese vendors, butchers, sweets shops, fishmongers, greengrocers, all merchants and purveyors of the produce that came in every day from all over Europe, delivered to me in Oxford. It was my Europe, Europe in the market stalls, Europe for sale in England and England itself a place of transition poised—glorified and run-down island, all in a single time zone—between America and the rest of Europe, an interlocutor, talking to both. (In 2012 Britain still maintains its own currency: no Euro there. A lover—white or near-white, American-born in any case—once told me I was Euro-trash, which remark I puzzle over yet.)

The history of cooking is the history of poetry. If you can read you can write; if you can write you can cook. I had won a poetry fellowship and was using it to buy time away from Ithaca and my job—I was an editor—and go to England with my wife and baby daughter to write for half a year. We lived on a tiny street in Jericho, Combe Road, by the Oxford Canal, by Port Meadow. This was the spring of 1987 and Jericho was not "gentrified" then and few people had telephones (or cars) and small grocery stores, called delis, were everywhere. Most delis were run by men or families from the Middle East but a few were operated by white Britons and I became aware, stepping into a couple of these, of the dislike for the colored foreigners whose stores I usually patronized for sudden necessities such as an egg, some cooking oil, or a bottle of beer. But I'd write in the morning and then put Madeline on my back and walk the

mile downtown to the Covered Market and look for dinner. The
deal for some time had been that I was cook because my wife was a
commuter but then she stopped commuting, a few months before
Madeline was born, and I continued as family cook for the next
twenty-five years at which point she unexpectedly called the mar-
riage off and left to find herself. And—as Robert Crumb said—she
took along a lunch.

In the mornings in Jericho I worked on a group of poems about
Birmingham, Alabama where my father had grown up. A song of
the south, the Old Country. Long hot days and nights. A jum-
ble of houses and train lines. The series—called "Look Ahead,
Look South," which was the advertising slogan for the Southern
Railroad—had to do with the deaths of my grandparents, my mem-
ories of that generation in that place. We'd take the evening train
from Dayton and arrive in Birmingham in the morning, detrain-
ing from the Pullman car, which was not segregated (money hav-
ing trumped that), into the South, which was. From my desk on
Combe Road I could see, if I craned my neck, the railroad across the
canal—many passenger trains each day and often, in the early eve-
ning, Madeline and I would cross the water on one bridge and then
walk to a second one over the tracks and wave to the drivers. In later
years I regaled her with stories of her life as a baby in Oxford and
during a time when she was in grade school and we were crossing
and re-crossing the border between Canada and the U.S. with some
frequency, she would threaten, from the back seat, to tell customs
that she'd been *born* in England. She has always enjoyed a joke.

In Birmingham my father learned how to cure hams from
his father. But my grandfather was no rustic peasant—he was,
like his son, my father, a physician. My grandfather had come to
Birmingham from Buff Bay, Portland Parish, Jamaica—he'd gone to
work, as a very young man, for United Fruit, saved money, and come
to the States to go to Clark and then to Meharry Medical College,
which produced many generations of black doctors; when my father
was a baby he'd left for a year—or possibly two years—to study anes-
thesiology at the University of Edinburgh. In 2012 the full text of

his 1923 article, "General Anesthesia," is available online. He died
in 1962, when I was eleven. We—my family—didn't raise our own
food but my father always had a garden, even in his last year, 2009,
which he spent in assisted living in Oakland, California.

(1962 at the edge of town)

No West Indians that I could see at my grandfather's funeral.

"Long lost relatives always eat a lot," sd my mother (meaning
just as well) on the ride to the graveyard at the furthest Negro
      edge
of Birmingham proper

—the city got lush in places then gave way
so descriptive shoulders of hills came into view over which
ranged pine trees & on a ridge, through those,

some white people went by on a train
(so near I could see them from where we stood under the
      canvas,
their pale arms & faces at the windows, clearly),

the pastoral looming up close as well,

"the mosaic of brightest southern colors"—it was that

for decades my grandfather was doctor too

to people out past the edge of town & took payment for that
in hams, in baskets of greens & fruit:

but all value is assigned, is brought in:

still, being the density & mirror both
was what I found confusing—

the fickle layers to endure, the worth standing in

In Oxford I began to read Elizabeth David. *French Provincial Cooking* took France to be a complex neighborhood, something to live *with* the way one unexpectedly might live anyplace and come to terms or familiarity with the complexity, even if the complexity does not "belong" to one. History of cooking? I learned to shop from my mother but I learned to cook in my twenties by reading the Rombauers, Craig Claiborne, and Julie Jordan's *Wings of Life* and that reading was adequate until I got to the Covered Market. The idea, for me, is not the *product* of cooking—some "authentic" or *coherent* example of cuisine, be the food on the plate fried chicken or coq au vin—but the articulated and social experience itself of the market with its essential (if occasionally luxurious, if occasionally unexpected) goods, its knowledgeable and hortatory shoppers and butchers, the experience gained over time by simple memory or familiarity, and, later, the "immediate experience" in the kitchen that cooking is.

Or cooking merges with situation. What's been on the back burner all this time? Who do you cook for? Where do you *go* to think about anything? If the idea is that the nature of the thing's separate from the thing's public status—meaning more contradictory and more immediate than that, though divorced from neither the cruelty of history nor the ambiguous quotidian—then nothing's captured or even tree'd in the kitchen. No clear voice emanates to set recipes or spice jars aright or guide stock pots to completion. The idea perhaps is to go on making things as one can without synthesizing—resisting, that is, the inclination to *gather* or to *fix*; the ideas—continuation, experience—are really rather simple.

Many years later, when she was a student at Cornell, Madeline would telephone from Wegmans with questions about cooking; in

November 2012, on a visit to Ithaca, I did my afternoon meditation
in a rented car parked inconspicuously on the Wegmans property—I
was the back burner itself, low heat, far edge of the lot.

3.

History of cooking. The big Kroger chain store on the West Side
was, in my memory of my own childhood, anomalous in that the
boundary between the corporate and local entrepreneurs was per-
meable—this is to say that in my memory people sold produce and
fish out of their cars and trucks in the parking lot. And it was at
a point of land as well, the situation where Wolf Creek meets the
Miami River—the two watercourses bounded the West Side, sep-
arated it from downtown to the east and the white Dayton View
neighborhood to the north. The railroad still follows Wolf Creek,
even in 2012, but in a story of *that* time—the 1950s—a freight train
on the line derailed one evening at the West Third Street crossing,
by the Kroger store, and the wood slats splintered on a livestock car
allowing pigs to escape into the West Side. A thousand pigs, a thou-
sand kitchens. Where did they go? Within half an hour—goes the
story—you couldn't find a single pig on the street. A man stopped
one of my father's patients and he had two pigs in the trunk of his
car and asked did my father's patient want to buy them.

　　The history of cooking is the history of poetry. Elizabeth David's
suggestion—to build the meal or the dish from its sources, to build
it among the simplicity of those—is basic to many situations, but
so is her understanding that French cuisine—be it provincial or
not—is a mark of "civilization." My arrival at the Covered Market,
French Provincial Cooking in hand, was incredibly unlikely, given
my antecedents. The story of the pigs is a twice or thrice told tale,
a story on the Negroes of the West Side passed around by those
Negroes or elements within the rather large and certainly socially
articulated group, less told to me than overheard by me as I'd listen,

as a child, to the talk of adults—that talk, the milieu, the range of speeches detailed what I elsewhere have called the contradictions of black life in Dayton. These contradictions constitute the tale of my tribe—that is, recognizable to some degree by rather many of us, a story such as that one will *move the crowd*, as I heard a black poet say once. Such movement is specific, particular. (In the writing *about* Sterling Brown's great poem, "Slim Greer," is no remark that I've found about the enormous self-consciousness of the ballad. In the poem, the title character—who, in spite of being the "Talkinges' guy / An biggest liar," does not narrate the piece—passes for white until he betrays himself by playing the piano well. Of great interest, at least to me, is the *frame*, established in the second stanza—there the effaced narrator says that Slim Greer,

> Tells a tale
> Of Arkansaw
> That keeps the kitchen
> In a roar . . .

Kitchens have got their color, my brothers, we must say so.) In 1987 I stepped from this to Europe and into the produce of Europe arrayed in gay profusion for me, a colored boy from the West Side. All bets were off, all roles were reversed—Europe was my playground, my market, my Sun City.

The heavy fiction is that the cook's voice—accurate, declamatory and familiar, revelatory—can be salvaged and that this would be a triumph, a "big idea." If we could hear James Hemings speaking to us from eighteenth-century France, the rift in state memory (I bow to Dr. Kissinger) could be closed; the healing process could begin. *If that don't fetch 'em*, sayeth the Duke, *I don't know Arkansaw.*

The context is always more telling. No ideas but in the various stacks and folds of that, and those are necessarily incomplete, open-ended. My ongoing narrative—the gate of my fiction—is my experience in the contexts of Babylon; my experience in the market stalls of the EEC was specific and particular but odd—in Oxford I was *unsummoned* but I studied French cuisine there and became, without intentional irony (but with time to practice and with the money to purchase available and high-quality foodstuffs), a passable cook. The delis of Jericho were operated (in the main) by colored people but shops in the Covered Market were staffed by white Britons—in 2012 the Lonely Planet website described it as "A haven of traditional butchers, fishmongers, cobblers, barbers," etc. and praised it also for its "traditional pies" and "traditional displays" of game at Christmas. I shopped it from someplace outside that; or, my baby girl on my back, I had crossed to it from someplace else.

WORKS CITED

G.P.V. and Helen Akrigg. *British Columbia Place Names* (Victoria: Sono Nis, 1988).

Herbert Aptheker. *The Negro in the American Revolution* (New York: International Publishers, 1940).

Harold Arlen and Johnny Mercer. "A Blues in the Night." 1941.

Margaret Atwood. *Surfacing* (New York: Simon & Schuster, 1972).

James Baldwin. *Notes of a Native Son* (Boston: Dial Press, 1963).

William Blake. *The Complete Poetry and Prose of William Blake* (New York: Anchor, 1997).

Donald Bogle. *Toms, Coons, Mulattoes, Mammies, and Bucks* (New York: Continuum, 1989).

Gwendolyn Brooks. *Blacks* (Chicago: David Company, 1989).

Sterling A. Brown. *The Collected Poems of Sterling A. Brown* (New York: Harper & Row, 1980).

Wallace Brown. "The Black Loyalists in Sierra Leone," in John W. Pulis, Ed., *Moving On: Black Loyalists in the Afro-Atlantic World* (New York: Garland Publishing, 1999).

Barry Cahill. "The Black Loyalist Myth in Atlantic Canada," *Acadiensis*, XXIX, 1 (Autumn 1999).

Ernest Camcroft. "Community Life Along the Grand Trunk Pacific System" in *Land, a Living, and Wealth, the Story of Farming & Social Conditions in Western Canada* (Winnipeg: Grand Trunk Pacific Railway, 1913).

George Elliott Clarke. *Fire on the Water, Volume One* (Lawrencetown Beach, N.S.: Pottersfield Press, 1999).

———. *Odysseys Home: Mapping African-Canadian Literature* (Toronto: University of Toronto Press, 2002).

Joseph Conrad. *Lord Jim* (New York: Signet Books, 1961).

Elizabeth David. *French Provincial Cooking*. (New York: Penguin Books, 1970).

W. E. B. Du Bois. *The Souls of Black Folk* (New York: Vintage / Library of America, 1990).

Robert Duncan. *The Opening of the Field* (New York: New Directions, 1960).

Bill Ellis. "'The Hook' Reconsidered: Problems in Classifying and Interpreting Adolescent Horror Legends" (*Folklore* 105, 1994).

Ralph Ellison. *Invisible Man* (New York: Vintage Books, 1989).

Linda Eversole. "John Robert Giscome: Jamaican Miner and Explorer." *British Columbia Historical News*, Spring 1985.

Sylvia Frey. *Water from the Rock* (Princeton: Princeton University Press, 1991).

Garbette Garroway. *Accomplishments and Contributions: A Handbook on Blacks in British Columbia* (Vancouver: Black Theatre West, 1990).

Henry Louis Gates, Jr. *Figures in Black* (New York: Oxford University Press, 1989).

Alan Gilbert. *Another Future: Poetry and Art in a Postmodern Twilight* (Wesleyan: Wesleyan U. P., 2006).

Paul Gilroy. *The Black Atlantic* (Cambridge: Harvard University Press, 1990).

John N. Grant. *Black Nova Scotians* (Halifax: Nova Scotia Museum: 1980).

Robert Ewell Greene. *Black Defenders of Freedom* (Chicago: Johnson Publishing Company, 1979).

Donna Haraway. *Simians, Cyborgs, and Women: The Reinvention of Nature* (New York; Routledge, 1991).

Lyn Hejinian. *The Language of Inquiry* (Berkeley: University of California Press, 2000).

Ernest Hemingway. *The Nick Adams Stories*. (New York: Scribner, 1981).

Herbert Hill. *Black Labor and the American Legal System: Race, Work, and the Law* (Madison: University of Wisconsin Press, 1985).

Allen and Albert Hughes (Directors). *Menace II Society* (Hollywood: New Line Cinema, 1993).

Edward Hoagland. *Notes From the Century Before* (San Francisco: North Point Press, 1982).

Langston Hughes. "Ask Your Mama: 13 Moods for Jazz" in *Collected Poems*, edited by Arnold Rampersad. (New York: Knopf 1994).

John Huston (Director). *The Treasure of Sierra Madre* (Hollywood: Warner Brothers, 1948).

Hal Jacobs. "'Blind Willie' McTell (1989–1959)," *The New Georgia Encyclopedia* (http://www.georgiaencyclopedia.org/nge/Article. jsp?id=h-875), 2009.

Rudyard Kipling. *Rudyard Kipling Illustrated* (New York: Avenel Books, 1982).

W. Kaye Lamb. "Some Notes on the Douglas Family" in *British Columbia Historical Quarterly*, 17, 1953.

Nella Larsen. *Passing* (New York: Penguin, 1997).

Robert Lowell. "For the Union Dead," in *For the Union Dead* (New York: Farrar, Straus, & Giroux, 1964).

Donna Lusitana (Director). "The Northern Frontier: Canadian West," segment of *The Real West* (Greystone Communications and Arts & Entertainment network, 1994).

Clarence Major. *From Juba to Jive: A Dictionary of African-American Slang* (New York: Penguin, 1994).

Bernadette Mayer. *Sonnets* (New York: Tender Buttons Books, 1989).

Carson McCullers. *Clock Without Hands* (Boston: Houghton Mifflin, 1953).

Willie McTell. "Statesboro Blues," quoted in Max Haymes, *Railroadin' Some: Railroads in the Early Blues* (York: Music Mentor Books, 2006).

A. G. Morice. *A History of the Northern Interior of British Columbia, Formerly New Caledonia* (Smithers: Northern Stationery Co., 1970).

Toni Morrison. *Playing in the Dark* (New York: Vintage, 1993).

Thylias Moss. "Interpretation of a Poem by Frost," in *Rainbow Remnants in a Rockbottom Ghetto Sky* (New York: Persea 1991).

Northeast Operating Rules Advisory Committee. *NORAC Operating Rules* (Conrail Operating Manuals, 2000).

Charles Olson. *The Maximus Poems*, ed. George Butterick (Berkeley: University of California Press, 1983).

Bridglal Pachai and Henry Bishop. *Historic Black Nova Scotia* (Halifax: Nimbus Publishing Company, 2006).

Benjamin Quarles. *The Negro in the American Revolution* (Chapel Hill: University of North Carolina Press, 1961).

Bruce Ramsey. *Ghost Towns of British Columbia* (Vancouver: Mitchell 1963).

Adam Roberts. Online review of *Duma Key* by Stephen King (Strange Horizons: http://www.strangehorizons.com/reviews/2008/02/duma_key_by_ste.shtml, 2008).

J. A. Rogers. *Sex and Race, Volume 1* (St. Petersburg, FL: Helga M. Rogers, 1984).

———. *Sex and Race, Volume 2* (St. Petersburg, FL: Helga M. Rogers, 1977).

Bernard Rose (Director). *Candyman* (Hollywood: PolyGram Filmed Entertainment, 1992).

Simon Schama. *Rough Crossings* (London: BBC Books, 2005).

Joseph Schott. *Rails Across Panama* (Indianapolis: Bobbs-Merrill, 1967).

Terry A. Slocum. *Thematic Cartography and Visualization* (Upper Saddle River, NJ: Prentice Hall 1999).

Wallace Stevens. *Opus Posthumous*, ed. Milton J. Bates (New York: Knopf, 1989).

———. "The Snowman," in *Collected Poems of Wallace Stevens* (New York: Knopf, 1954).

Mark Twain. *The Adventures of Huckleberry Finn* (New York: W. W. Norton, 1962).

James W. St.G. Walker. *The Black Loyalists* (New York: Africana Publishing Company / Holmes and Meier Publishing: 1976).

————. "Myth, History and Revisionism: The Black Loyalists Revisited," *Acadiensis*, XXIX, 1 (Autumn 1999).

Orson Welles (Director). *Touch of Evil* (Hollywood: Universal Studios,1958).

Walt Whitman. *Leaves of Grass* (New York: Bantam Classics, 1983).

Sherley Anne Williams. *Some One Sweet Angel Chile* (New York: Morrow, 1982).

Ellen Gibson Wilson. *The Loyal Blacks* (New York: Capricorn/ Putnam's, 1976).

Robin Winks. *The Blacks in Canada* (New Haven: Yale University Press, 1967).

James Wright. *Collected Poems* (Wesleyan, CT: Wesleyan University Press, 1971).

Richard Wright. *Native Son* (New York: Harper & Row, 1966).

Howard Zinn. *A People's History of the United States* (New York: Harper Collins, 1990).

C. S. GISCOMBE is the author of several books of poetry, including *Giscome Road*, *Prairie Style* and *Here*, all three of which are also available from Dalkey Archive Press. He has also published a memoir entitled *Into and Out of Dislocation*. He is the editor of *Mixed Blood*, a poetry journal, and teaches at the University of California at Berkeley.